TECHNOLOGY

PHIL GATES

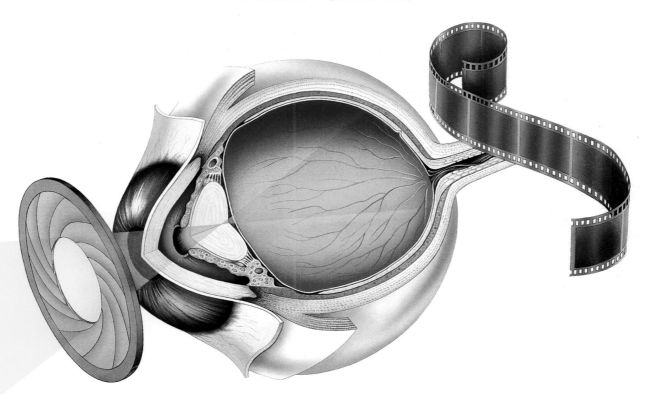

Kingfisher

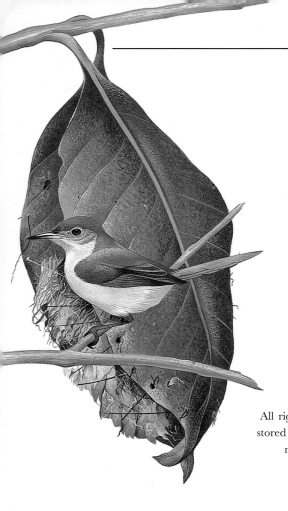

KINGFISHER
An imprint of Larousse plc
Elsley House, 24–30 Great Titchfield Street,
London W1P 7AD
First published in paperback by Kingfisher 1997
2 4 6 8 10 9 7 5 3 1
First published in hardback by Kingfisher 1995

A CIP catalogue for this book is available from the
British Library.

ISBN: 0 7534 0150 9

Printed in Hong Kong
Editor: Catherine Headlam
Designers: Shaun Barlow, Karin Ambrose,
John Jamieson and Terry Woodley
Art Editor: Sue Aldworth
Picture Research: Elaine Willis
With thanks to Dr Huw Edwards

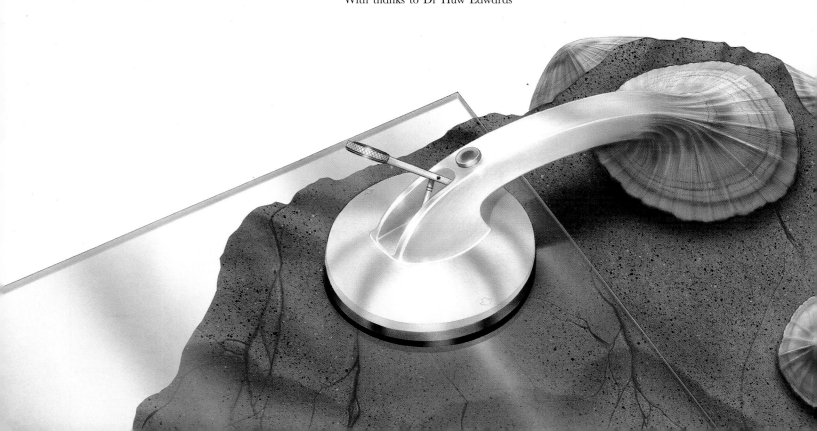

CONTENTS

◀ A dandelion seed's hairy parachute slows its fall to the ground in the same way that a parachute slows the fall of a person.

▶ The rattlesnake's rattle is a natural alarm that keeps intruders away. People put burglar alarms on buildings in order to warn intruders to keep away.

Wild TECHNOLOGY

Ever since humans first walked on the surface of Earth, the plants and animals around us have filled our minds with ideas. Many of our best inventions are copied from, or already in use by, other living things.

We have only discovered a tiny fraction of the vast numbers of living organisms that share our planet. Somewhere, amongst the millions of organisms that remain undiscovered, there are natural inventions that could improve our lives. They could provide new medicines, building materials, ways of controlling pests and dealing with pollution. This is why it is so important to protect and conserve the living world.

Our world is changing quickly. Survival may depend on protecting and learning from the plants and animals that have lived through even greater changes in the past.

Phil Gates.

▲ *Large colonies of giant tube worms have been discovered deep in the ocean around undersea volcanoes, They contain strange bacteria that allow them to live on sulphur and to survive in hot water and total darkness. The bacteria are now being used to develop new chemical processes.*

The complex network of ribs on the underside of the giant water lily supports its large surface area. These ribs have been copied in buildings, most famously by Joseph Paxton in the Crystal Palace.

1

DESIGN FOR USE
LIVING STRUCTURES

Life is a natural experiment that began 3.5 billion years ago on Earth and is still in progress.

During this period evolution has produced a huge variety of structural adaptations in living organisms. Evolution is the gradual process by which all living things have changed since life first began*. These adaptations have been tested in a natural laboratory that has exposed them to the most extreme physical conditions. The organisms that exist today do so because they are descendants of others that carried adaptations which allow them to survive fire, ice ages, typhoons, drought, and even catastrophes caused by asteroid impacts. It makes sense to copy the best features of their evolutionary design for our own use.

Giant water lily leaves.

No structural designs that are purely human inventions have ever been tested so thoroughly. The plant kingdom contains giant redwood trees that are the largest living things that have ever occurred on Earth's surface. The strength of the wood that supports their 100-metre tall trunks depends on bundles of microscopic tubes that are glued together to provide strength and stability. The success of living organisms lies in the design and assembly of their smallest components.

The Crystal Palace, London.

For further explanation of 'evolution' and other difficult words, see the glossary on page 76.

TROPICAL TREE TO CATHEDRAL
STRUCTURE

Large, complex structures must have internal strengthening, to counteract the forces that will act upon them when they are in use. Strength can come from choice of materials, because some materials are stronger than others, or from the ways in which the materials are formed into parts and assembled. Cross bracing and other methods of load distribution are common in animals and plants.

▼ *An aeroplane's weight must be kept to a minimum and the wings must be especially strong. Wings are made from a series of ribs connected by spars and covered with a metal skin, producing a very light and strong structure.*

Rib

Spar

The bone of a bird

TROPICAL TREE
Tropical rain forest trees may be over 50 metres tall and have a heavy crown of branches and foliage. When high winds strike the tops of the trees, enormous forces are transmitted to the base of the trunk and roots. But the tree is stabilized by great wooden buttresses that broaden its base, stiffen its lower trunk and act as stabilizers.

▲ *Birds must be as light as possible, in order to reduce the energy needed for flight. Many of their bones are filled with air spaces, but their rigidity is maintained by internal trusses and struts. This construction produces a good compromise between minimum weight and maximum strength.*

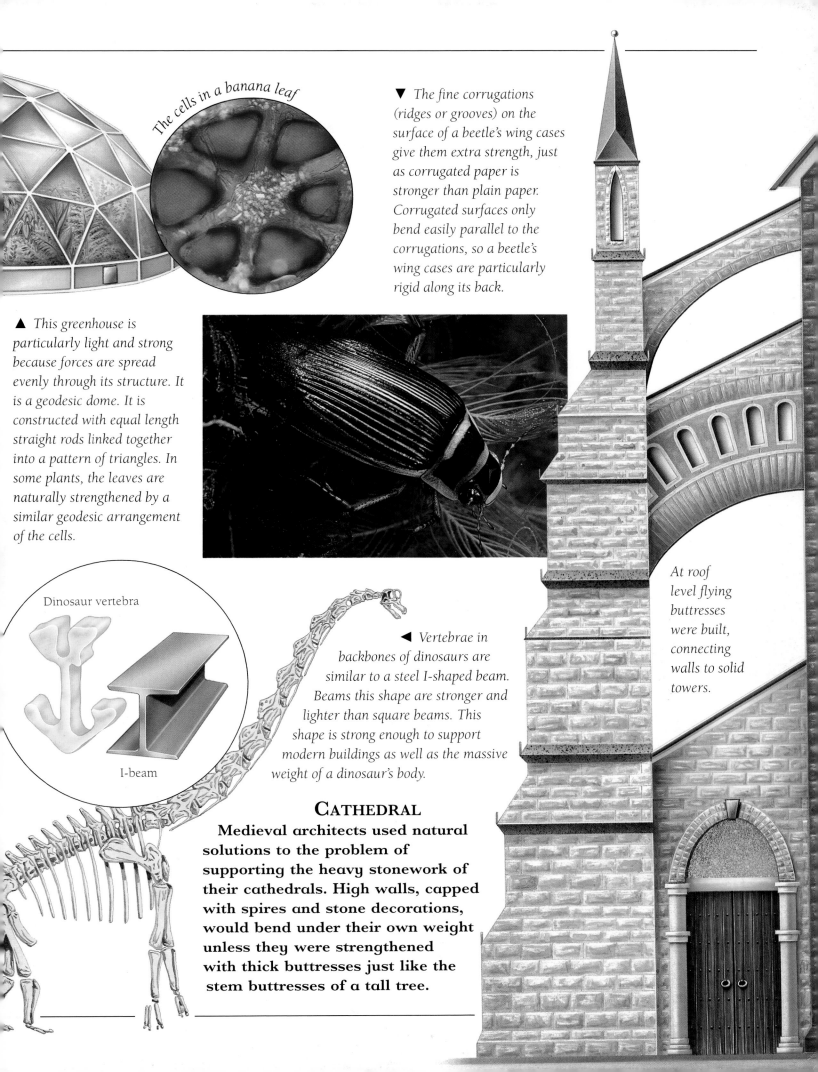

The cells in a banana leaf

▼ *The fine corrugations (ridges or grooves) on the surface of a beetle's wing cases give them extra strength, just as corrugated paper is stronger than plain paper. Corrugated surfaces only bend easily parallel to the corrugations, so a beetle's wing cases are particularly rigid along its back.*

▲ *This greenhouse is particularly light and strong because forces are spread evenly through its structure. It is a geodesic dome. It is constructed with equal length straight rods linked together into a pattern of triangles. In some plants, the leaves are naturally strengthened by a similar geodesic arrangement of the cells.*

Dinosaur vertebra

I-beam

◄ *Vertebrae in backbones of dinosaurs are similar to a steel I-shaped beam. Beams this shape are stronger and lighter than square beams. This shape is strong enough to support modern buildings as well as the massive weight of a dinosaur's body.*

At roof level flying buttresses were built, connecting walls to solid towers.

CATHEDRAL

Medieval architects used natural solutions to the problem of supporting the heavy stonework of their cathedrals. High walls, capped with spires and stone decorations, would bend under their own weight unless they were strengthened with thick buttresses just like the stem buttresses of a tall tree.

LIMPET
TO SUCTION CUP
GRIPPING

Good grip is essential in everyday life for all land animals. We need grip to walk on surfaces where there is little friction or to handle smooth or wet objects. Grooved treads on shoes and tyres, non-slip treads on the edges of stairs, and ribbed handles on tools and bicycle handlebars are all designed to provide a better grip.

▲ *Snowshoe hares have hairy mats on the soles of their feet, which help to spread their weight and stop their feet sinking in soft snow. The snowshoes worn by trappers in the Arctic work in exactly the same way – by spreading their weight over a wide area.*

LIMPET

Limpets are molluscs that live on exposed sea shores. They avoid being swept away by waves, or being dried out by the sun at low tide, by attaching themselves to rocks. They do this with a large, muscular foot that creates a powerful suction force, drawing the limpet down onto the rock surface. At high tide the limpets creep over the rocks and feed, but when the tide goes out they withdraw into their shells and seal themselves to the rock surface.

Suckers on the octopus' tentacles can grip its prey strongly.

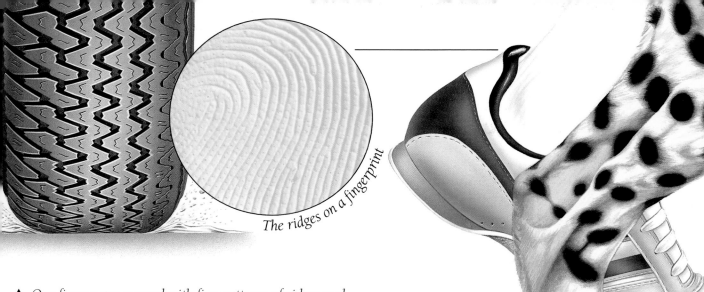

The ridges on a fingerprint

▲ *Our fingers are covered with fine patterns of ridges and grooves, which help us to grip smooth, slippery objects. The tread pattern on a tyre is a larger version of the same adaptation, to ensure that the tyre grips wet roads.*

SUCTION CUP

Suction cups are like mechanical limpets and are ideal for moving some awkward materials. Handling large sheets of glass, with their smooth surfaces and sharp edges, can be dangerous. So the cup is stuck onto the glass surface and held in place by suction, allowing the glass to be moved without breakage or injury. A single person can pick up a large sheet of glass with a pair of suction cups and place it carefully in a window frame.

▲ *Cheetahs, which chase their prey at up to 100 kilometres an hour, have long, permanently extended claws to help them grip loose surfaces. The sharp spikes on running shoes give a sprinter a good grip on the athletics track.*

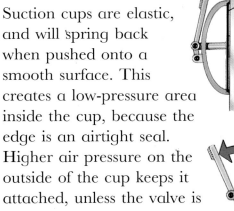

SUCTION PRESSURE

Suction cups are elastic, and will spring back when pushed onto a smooth surface. This creates a low-pressure area inside the cup, because the edge is an airtight seal. Higher air pressure on the outside of the cup keeps it attached, unless the valve is opened to let the air pressures inside and outside become equal again and then the cup will lift off.

Elastic cup

1 Suction cup placed on glass

2 Lever pulls elastic cup creating suction

Low-pressure area

BURR TO ZIP
SECURE FASTENINGS

When we get dressed we use a variety of temporary fastenings to keep our clothes in place. Shoelaces and buckles, and buttons for clothes have been used for thousands of years, but two modern inventions – the zip-fastener and Velcro – have made dressing faster and easier. Both inventions depend on joining objects with small hooks and draw inspiration from the same processes in nature, where efficient flight in birds and the spreading of plant seeds both make use of the same technique.

▲ *The flight feathers of birds generate lift when air flows over their smooth surface. Each feather is made up of thousands of fine branches, called barbules, arranged along a central shaft. Every barbule has rows of microscopic hooks which interlock so that the feather has a flat, rigid surface.*

The barbules of a feather

Central shaft of feather

Slide

ZIP FASTENER

A zip uses a slide with wedges inside it to force the teeth apart, or back together. The teeth are hooked so that they interlock to fasten securely. Birds' feathers have hooked barbules which often separate during flight. Birds preen the feathers, pulling them through their beak, to join the hooks together again.

▼ *Large flat wings are efficient but cannot be folded away easily to protect them. Bees solve this problem by having two pairs of wings, joined by a row of fine hooks, called a hamulus. When the insect lands, the hamulus is disconnected and the wings can be folded neatly along the bee's back.*

The hamulus of an insect's wing

▼ *Velcro makes a very efficient fastening for bags, clothes and also shoes.*

THE VELCRO STORY

In 1957 burdock provided the inspiration for the invention of Velcro, by the Swiss engineer George de Mestral. He found burrs clinging to his clothes and noticed that they were covered in fine hooks. He then spent eight years developing Velcro, a synthetic material made from two nylon strips. One strip is covered with tiny loops and the other is coated with minute hooks. When they are pressed together they stick firmly, but they can be instantly ripped apart. The name 'Velcro' comes from the French for velvet (**vel**ours) and hook (**cro**chet).

All plants need to spread, or disperse, their seeds so that the seedlings can colonize new areas and avoid over-crowding. Many plants, including herb bennet, agrimony, and goose-grass rely on burrs for seed dispersal. The burrs get caught in animals' fur and people's clothing. By the time the seeds fall out of the burr, they will have been carried far away.

The hooks of a burr

BURR

A burr is covered with hundreds of small, sharp hooks. Burdock, a member of the thistle family, is one of many plants that sheds its seeds in hooked seedheads (burrs).

Animals that live in colonies
often build homes of many
compartments. In this
organism, Flustra, each
compartment contains a tiny
animal like a sea anemone.
The whole organism is like a
large apartment building.

2
USING NATURAL MATERIALS
BUILDING

The earliest humans sheltered from bad weather and danger by living in caves. Many of the best-preserved ancient human remains have been found in limestone caverns. As the human population increased, it must have become more difficult to find suitable homes. Instead, groups of hunters would have built simple, temporary homes from the natural materials that were available.

They probably copied animal building methods, using wood, dried grasses and mud. These are often used by birds for nests and do not produce long-lasting buildings. As permanent towns and cities grew up, people began to try stronger construction materials, such as mud bricks.

Modern buildings are often constructed from many identical compartments, or rooms.

Some animals make harder materials, for example, termites make a natural concrete, while coral organisms extract calcium salts from sea water to make

A coral reef

limestone reefs that are hard enough to rip open a steel ship's hull. As cities and buildings grew larger, human builders have experimented with mixtures of similar ingredients to produce the reinforced concrete that allows us to build skyscrapers.

Now, our buildings are so warm and secure that we face a continuous problem of keeping out other animals such as mice, rats, birds, wasps, spiders, cockroaches, moths and even termites.

NESTS TO POTTERY
NATURAL MATERIALS

Natural materials, like stone, bone, clay and plant fibres were the only materials available to the first human cultures. Simple methods of weaving and pottery soon developed into more complicated ones as advanced civilizations developed.

Animals build nests to provide a sheltered place to breed and to protect themselves and their young from predators. Temporary nests are usually made from light, strong materials such as grass stems, which are easy to collect but decay quickly. Permanent homes are often made from wood or mud and are added to, until they become massive structures that survive for years.

▲ *Indian tailor birds build nests by stitching living leaves together. They thread dry grass stems through the edges of the leaves, creating a nest that is hidden in the foliage.*

▲ *The weaver birds of Africa are instinctive basket makers. Their nests are made from woven grass stems that are attached to a tree with a light grass frame. The first nests that young weaver birds make often fall apart and they need to practice until they perfect their weaving technique.*

Chipboard

PAPER MAKING
People make paper by treating logs of wood to make pulp which can then be squeezed out into sheets. Wasps are the natural inventors of paper making. They build nests from shreds of chewed wood, mixed with their saliva. Chipboard is a similar material, except that the wasp's saliva is replaced with artificial glue.

▶ *A skilled potter can spin a shapeless lump of wet clay on a potter's wheel and convert it into an elegant and useful pot.*

The paper nest of a wasp

▶ *Green tree ants hold their grubs in their jaws and use the sticky, silken threads that are produced by the grubs' ends to weave leaves together, to make a nest. Cloth and carpets are woven by passing threads under and over each other. using a piece of wood, called a shuttle, with thread attached. The green tree ants are using their grubs as living shuttles to weave their nest from leaves.*

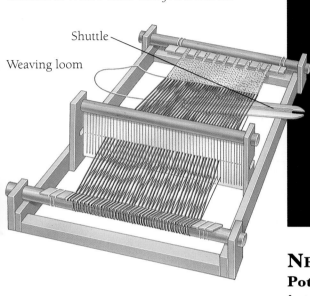

Shuttle

Weaving loom

POTTERY

Pottery is made from clay. Clay consists of wet soil particles that can be moulded into shapes and then baked in a kiln. The earliest human potters probably built up wet clay into a pot, using much the same method as the potter wasp. Then, over 700 years ago, potters in China developed technologies for baking clay at high temperatures to produce fine porcelain such as we use now.

NESTS

Potter wasps collect wet clay and mould it into a nest that can be used after it has dried in the heat of the Sun. Nests made from mud do not rot (decay) and survive long after the young have hatched. House martins, which are birds that make mud nests often use the same nest for several years, with a few minor repairs.

▼ *Piles of rotting plant materials become warm if the heat they produce cannot escape. The layers need to be mixed regularly, so that they decay evenly and maintain a steady temperature.*

FUNGUS GARDENS TO COMPOST HEAPS
COMPOSTING FOR HEAT

Rotting plant material produces heat. Some animals and people build 'compost heaps' to use this heat. When plants die they are broken down by fungi and bacteria that digest and use the remains for their own growth. This process of digestion releases heat energy. If the plant material is piled in a heap the heat is trapped inside, in a process called composting. Some animals exploit this natural system to keep their eggs warm.

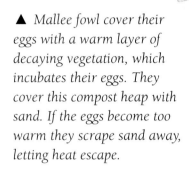

▲ *Mallee fowl cover their eggs with a warm layer of decaying vegetation, which incubates their eggs. They cover this compost heap with sand. If the eggs become too warm they scrape sand away, letting heat escape.*

COMPOST HEAPS
Compost heaps must be constructed from layers of plant material with different textures, allowing oxygen to reach the fungi and bacteria that attack the dead plants. When decay begins the heap warms up and the rotting process becomes faster, but if the heap becomes too hot the bacteria and fungi are killed. Gardeners often build compost heaps to provide rich decayed plant material to spread on their soil. The warmth of a compost heap sometimes attracts cold-blooded reptiles, such as grass snakes and slow-worms.

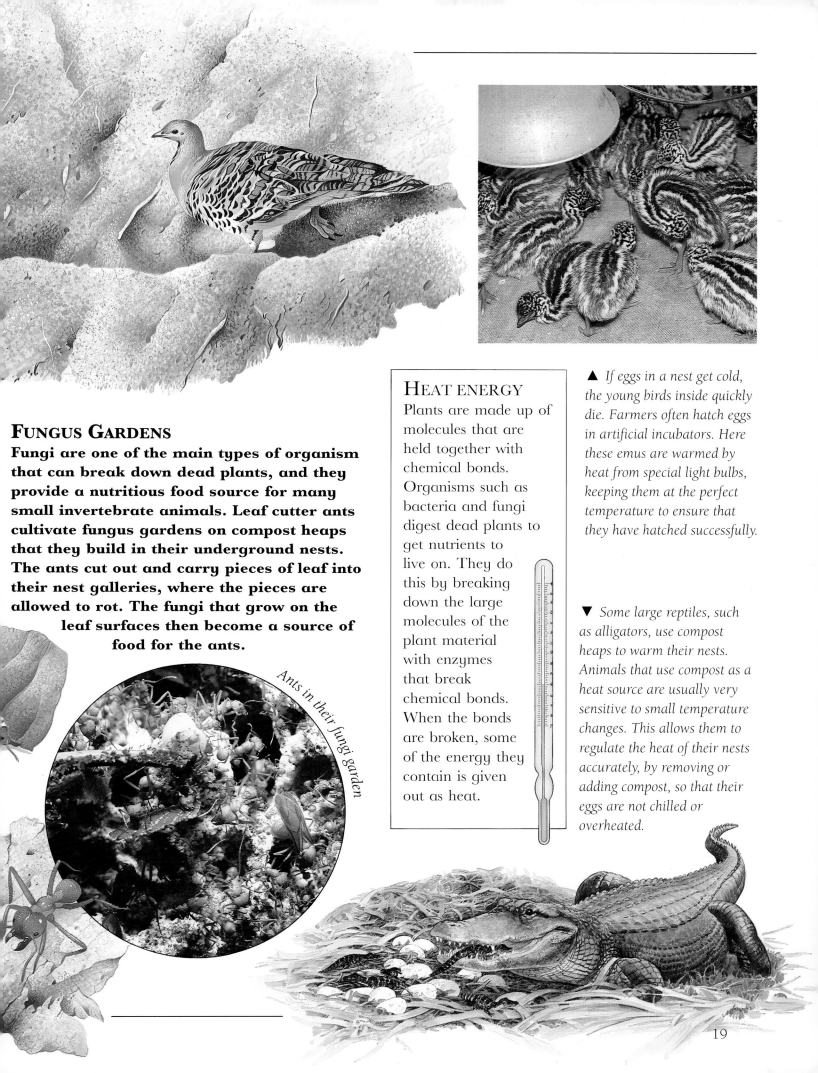

FUNGUS GARDENS

Fungi are one of the main types of organism that can break down dead plants, and they provide a nutritious food source for many small invertebrate animals. Leaf cutter ants cultivate fungus gardens on compost heaps that they build in their underground nests. The ants cut out and carry pieces of leaf into their nest galleries, where the pieces are allowed to rot. The fungi that grow on the leaf surfaces then become a source of food for the ants.

Ants in their fungi garden

HEAT ENERGY

Plants are made up of molecules that are held together with chemical bonds. Organisms such as bacteria and fungi digest dead plants to get nutrients to live on. They do this by breaking down the large molecules of the plant material with enzymes that break chemical bonds. When the bonds are broken, some of the energy they contain is given out as heat.

▲ If eggs in a nest get cold, the young birds inside quickly die. Farmers often hatch eggs in artificial incubators. Here these emus are warmed by heat from special light bulbs, keeping them at the perfect temperature to ensure that they have hatched successfully.

▼ Some large reptiles, such as alligators, use compost heaps to warm their nests. Animals that use compost as a heat source are usually very sensitive to small temperature changes. This allows them to regulate the heat of their nests accurately, by removing or adding compost, so that their eggs are not chilled or overheated.

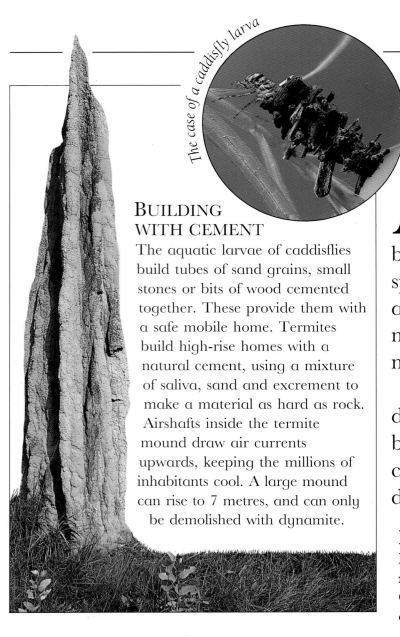

BUILDING WITH CEMENT

The aquatic larvae of caddisflies build tubes of sand grains, small stones or bits of wood cemented together. These provide them with a safe mobile home. Termites build high-rise homes with a natural cement, using a mixture of saliva, sand and excrement to make a material as hard as rock. Airshafts inside the termite mound draw air currents upwards, keeping the millions of inhabitants cool. A large mound can rise to 7 metres, and can only be demolished with dynamite.

PRAIRIE DOGS TO CHANNEL TUNNEL
EARTH ENGINEERING

Animals that live in tunnels are hidden from many predators, but building underground requires special skills. Tunnels must be level and parallel to the surface. They must not flood or collapse, and they must have fresh air.

Even for human builders, large dams and high-rise buildings only became possible when reinforced concrete construction methods were devised during the 20th century.

PRAIRIE DOGS

Prairie dogs are social animals that excavate massive networks of interconnecting tunnels. Good air circulation is essential, so the prairie dogs build volcano-shaped ventilation towers. These help to draw currents of air through their underground cities.

◀ *Humans build dams to create large lakes that contain millions of litres of water. This large store of water is used in homes, factories and farms. It can also be used to provide energy that is converted into electricity.*

▲ *Beavers dam small streams, creating ponds where they build a lodge of logs and turf, to create an ideal home for their family groups. Their dams are so well engineered that they can last for centuries.*

CHANNEL TUNNEL

The Channel Tunnel is one of the greatest engineering projects of the 20th century. It provides a high-speed rail service between Britain and France that can carry passengers and freight. Ventilation systems ensure that no poisonous and explosive gases build up, and that the air is kept dry and clean.

▼ *Air is drawn through tunnels by creating an area of lower pressure in one place. Air then moves towards this area and the air flows in the tunnel. In tunnels built by people fans are used to draw the air through. Prairie dogs and termites build towers, because air moving over the top of these mounds draws the air currents up their tunnels providing ventilation.*

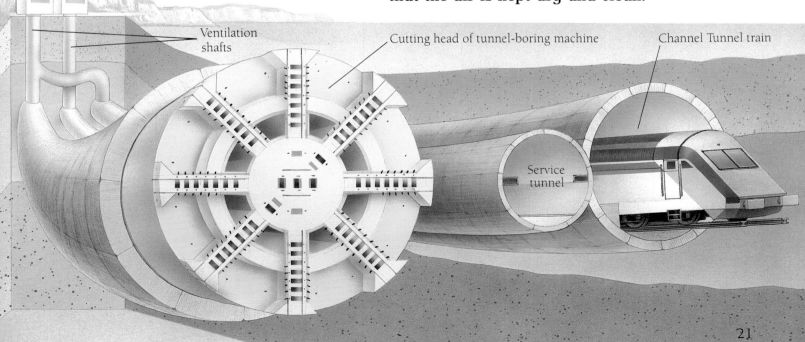

Ventilation shafts

Cutting head of tunnel-boring machine

Channel Tunnel train

Service tunnel

Unrelated organisms often find the same solutions to similar problems independently. This process, known as convergent evolution, has led to the close resemblance between the defensive scales of a pine cone and a pangolin.

3
KEEPING
ENEMIES AWAY
DEFENCE

Living organisms defend themselves from two kinds of threat. Firstly, the threat of being eaten, for example, plants, animals and people are part of food chains, in which herbivores eat plants and then carnivores eat herbivores.

Secondly, animals face war-like threats from their own species, when there are disputes over territory and possessions.

Some animals rely on speed to reduce the risk of becoming a predator's meal, and quickly run away. Plants and slow-moving animals must use an alternative strategy, and often defend themselves with sharp spines or thick armour, making it more difficult for a predator to damage or injure them. Armour of all kinds is awkward and cumbersome, so many species hide from predators instead, relying on camouflage patterns.

Pine cone

When animals are cornered by a predator their only option is to fight back. Then, hungry attackers will sometimes look for an easier meal, instead of risking severe injury in a fight. Fights involve risks for both attacker and defender, so many confrontations are settled instead with threat displays. Animals with defensive weapons often combine them with threatening behaviour and warning colours, so that an enemy that has been defeated once will remember to avoid another damaging fight in future. Plants often use foul-tasting poisons to deter grazing animals such as rabbits, which soon learn to avoid plants that make them ill.

The scales of a pangolin provide flexible armour.

ARMADILLO TO ARMOURED CAR
ARMOUR

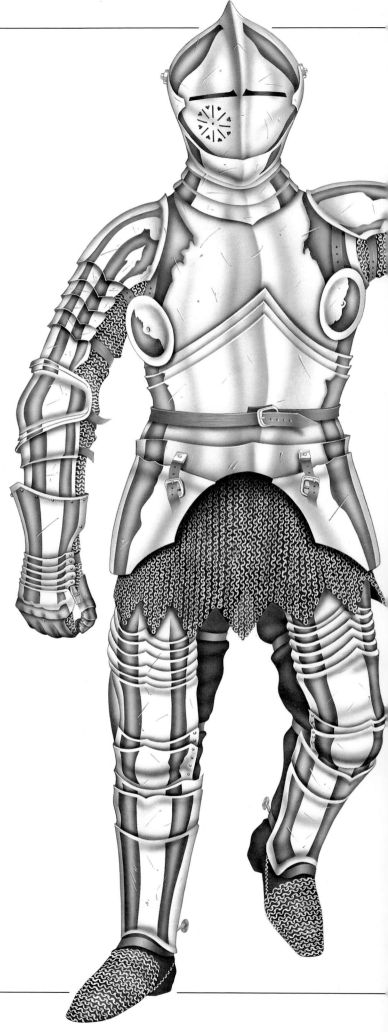

Thick, heavy armour can protect animals and people from attack, but it can make its owner slow and clumsy. Large sheets of rigid armour also restrict movement and, in more mobile animals, are replaced by systems of small over-lapping plates or scales, which provide flexible protection. Many animals have evolved armour that only covers their most vulnerable parts as a compromise between the advantages of reduced weight and easy movement, and the disadvantage of reduced protection.

ARMADILLO
The back of an armadillo is protected by overlapping armoured plates of bone, connected by softer skin. These provide enough flexibility for the animal to move fast and easily. When the animal is attacked its flexible armour allows it to roll up, protecting its soft underparts, head and legs, inside a ball of armour plate.

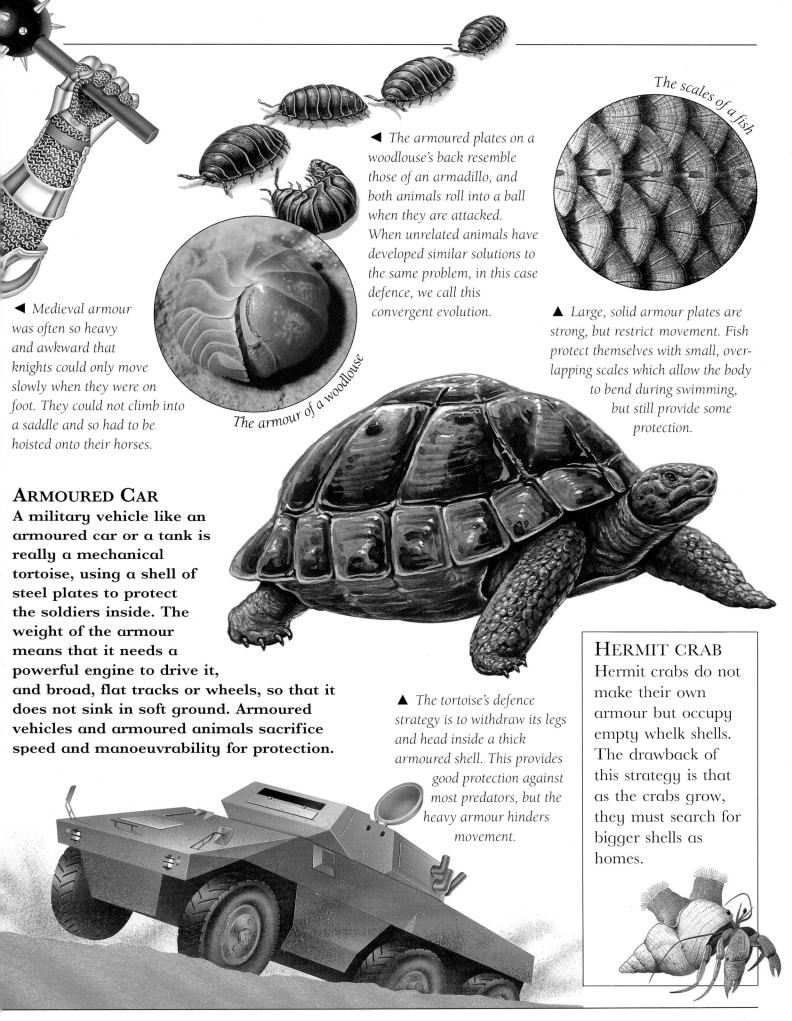

◄ *The armoured plates on a woodlouse's back resemble those of an armadillo, and both animals roll into a ball when they are attacked. When unrelated animals have developed similar solutions to the same problem, in this case defence, we call this convergent evolution.*

The scales of a fish

◄ *Medieval armour was often so heavy and awkward that knights could only move slowly when they were on foot. They could not climb into a saddle and so had to be hoisted onto their horses.*

The armour of a woodlouse

▲ *Large, solid armour plates are strong, but restrict movement. Fish protect themselves with small, over-lapping scales which allow the body to bend during swimming, but still provide some protection.*

ARMOURED CAR

A military vehicle like an armoured car or a tank is really a mechanical tortoise, using a shell of steel plates to protect the soldiers inside. The weight of the armour means that it needs a powerful engine to drive it, and broad, flat tracks or wheels, so that it does not sink in soft ground. Armoured vehicles and armoured animals sacrifice speed and manoeuvrability for protection.

▲ *The tortoise's defence strategy is to withdraw its legs and head inside a thick armoured shell. This provides good protection against most predators, but the heavy armour hinders movement.*

HERMIT CRAB

Hermit crabs do not make their own armour but occupy empty whelk shells. The drawback of this strategy is that as the crabs grow, they must search for bigger shells as homes.

ROSES TO RAZOR WIRE

SPINES AND SPIKES

The spines of a cactus

Sharp spines deter most predators by increasing the risk of injury during an attack. The painful wounds that they inflict often become infected and can even be fatal, so predators approach animals that have spiny weapons with great caution. Long spines ensure that a predator keeps its distance, but they also restrict the movement of their owner. Like many natural defensive structures, the ideal spine length is a compromise between maximum protection and the inconvenience it causes to its owner when not in use.

The thorns of a rose

▲ *Cacti store water in their stems and so could be a major source of food and water for desert animals. They protect themselves against grazing animals with the needle-sharp thorns that replace their leaves.*

ROSES

Plants cannot run away from their enemies, so they often use spines to deter grazing animals that would otherwise eat them. If the stems of spiny plants are cut down the new growth that replaces them often develops an even denser covering of spines, increasing protection against future attack. Thorns are usually formed from modified leaves that have become woody and sharp.

The spikes of barbed wire

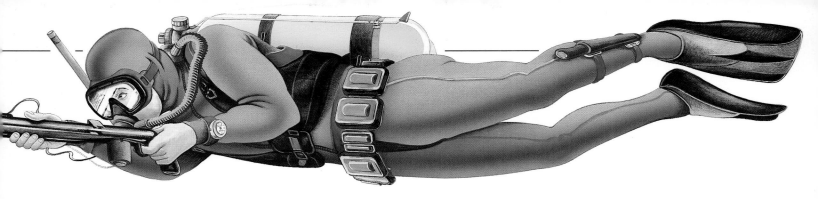

▲ *A diver sometimes needs protection when exploring under water. He or she will use a gun that fires a harpoon, fixed to a long line, to protect themselves from any dangerous fish.*

SHOOTING SPINES

Sea anemones can fire needle-sharp spines into their attackers. The anemone's tentacles are covered with cells called nematocysts, which contain coiled, barbed threads that shoot out with lightning speed when another animal brushes against tiny trigger hairs that cover their surface. When triggered, the nematocysts turn inside out to reveal their spines. If you touch a sea anemone's tentacles they feel sticky, because the barbs on their nematocyst harpoons catch in your skin, but they are so small that they cannot penetrate it.

▲ *The sea urchin's defence is simple. Enemies that attack are kept at bay by a ball of needle-sharp spines, any of which may break off and inflict painful wounds.*

▼ *Porcupines are rodents that live on the ground. They have long curved claws that are ideal for burrowing but which make them clumsy runners. If they are attacked in the open, porcupines can defend themselves by raising their quills and charging backwards into their enemies. The quills break off easily and create wounds that become infected.*

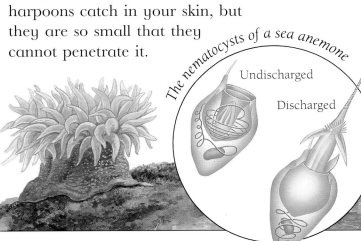

The nematocysts of a sea anemone

Undischarged

Discharged

RAZOR WIRE

Barbed wire was originally designed to make quick, cheap fences that would stop domestic animals from wandering away. It has the same effect as a barrier of thorny roses or spiny cacti. Barbed wire is now also used to protect buildings against intruders, trapping anyone who tries to push their way through its razor-covered coils and wounding them.

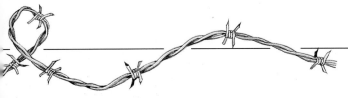

RATTLES TO BURGLAR ALARMS
WARNING NOISES

Most poisonous animals only attack as a last line of defence, unless they are looking for food. Any aggressive confrontation that leads to a fight may end in serious injury to both attacker and defender, so warnings and threats are often used instead. Loud or menacing noises, such as hisses, screams, barks, yells and growls are all sounds that are used as part of threat displays, as a danger warning.

BURGLAR ALARMS

Often people protect their homes against burglars by using loud alarm bells. Hidden switches inside the house set off the alarm if someone enters. The presence of an alarm bell on the outside of a house warns burglars that a loud noise will draw attention to them if they try to break in.

RATTLES

Rattlesnakes are well camouflaged, and risk being accidentally trodden underfoot by large animals. If an animal gets too close, the snake shakes a loud rattle on its tail, which frightens the intruder away. This alarm ensures that the snake does not waste its poisonous bite on an animal too large to eat.

▼ *Bird scarers that broadcast recorded distress calls from frightened birds are a harmless way to scare bird pests away from fruit trees in orchards. The alarming sounds from the loudspeakers convince all the birds that they are under attack.*

INKCLOUD TO SMOKESCREEN

CHEMICALS

▲ *Some species of cobra can defend themselves by squirting poison from the glands in their mouth.*

INKCLOUD

Sometimes chemical defences can create confusion. Octopus and cuttlefish have ink sacs full of dye. If they are attacked they squirt a cloud of dye into the water, then escape quickly, hidden from enemies by their chemical smokescreen.

Mechanical defences, like armour and spines, can be very effective but can also hinder their owner. Chemical defences are compact and far more convenient because they are only used when their owner is actually attacked. They can usually be quickly replaced, unlike damaged mechanical defences. Animals' chemical deterrents are so effective that they have been copied by humans – police forces sometimes quell riots by spraying the people with irritant chemicals, such as tear-gas, and in some cities individuals may carry special sprays to defend themselves from attack.

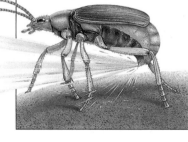

SMOKESCREEN

In wartime the element of surprise is very important, so soldiers may move into battle under cover of a dense smokescreen.

29

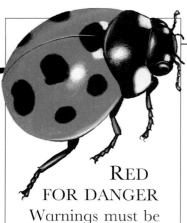

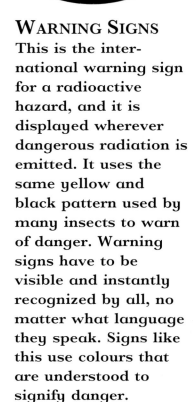

WASPS TO WARNING SIGNS
USING COLOUR

RED FOR DANGER
Warnings must be understood by all. Birds know that red ladybirds produce foul-tasting poisons. All drivers know what a red traffic light means.

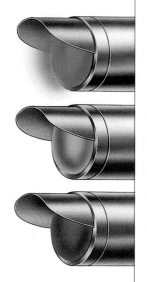

Colour can be used as a method of defence in two different ways. If an animal is poisonous and can bite or sting, then bright conspicuous colours can act as a warning to potential enemies that they may be injured or killed if they approach too closely. Predators soon learn to associate certain easily-recognized colour schemes with danger. Humans often use colour in a similar way to warn of hazards, for example, by using striped barriers at railway level crossings, and brightly coloured warning symbols on dangerous objects or substances.

WARNING SIGNS
This is the international warning sign for a radioactive hazard, and it is displayed wherever dangerous radiation is emitted. It uses the same yellow and black pattern used by many insects to warn of danger. Warning signs have to be visible and instantly recognized by all, no matter what language they speak. Signs like this use colours that are understood to signify danger.

WASPS
Wasps are armed with poisonous stings. They also have characteristic black and yellow stripes, which act as a warning to other animals. These warning markings are common among animals, and many different species that are only distantly related also carry similar patterns and colour combinations of yellow and black, or black and red. This means that predators always associate these markings with danger, even if their owners are harmless. Hoverflies have no sting, but copy the colours of wasps, and this similarity protects them.

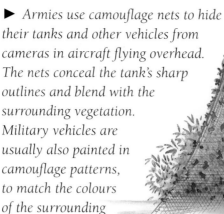

► Armies use camouflage nets to hide their tanks and other vehicles from cameras in aircraft flying overhead. The nets conceal the tank's sharp outlines and blend with the surrounding vegetation. Military vehicles are usually also painted in camouflage patterns, to match the colours of the surrounding landscape.

▲ South American poison dart frogs produce some of the world's most deadly poisons in their skin. One animal carries enough poison to kill 1,500 people. The bright colours of these little frogs serve as a constant warning to all other animals to leave them alone.

◄ The mottled feathers of a frogmouth make it almost impossible to find among the branches. The success of its camouflage often depends on it remaining perfectly still.

▼ Flower mantids sit perfectly still amongst the flowers on plants. They are so well concealed that butterflies mistake them for flower petals. Then, once the butterfly lands on the flower and it is too late for it to escape, the mantid grabs its prey.

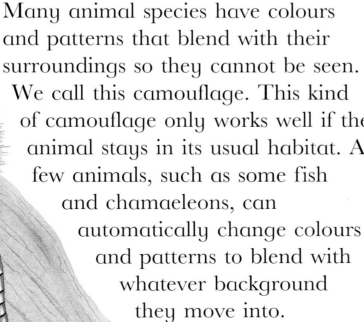

Many animal species have colours and patterns that blend with their surroundings so they cannot be seen. We call this camouflage. This kind of camouflage only works well if the animal stays in its usual habitat. A few animals, such as some fish and chamaeleons, can automatically change colours and patterns to blend with whatever background they move into.

Insects and birds evolved the power of flight separately, millions of years ago. Most moths have flat wings but this plume moth's wings resemble birds' feathers – an example of different organisms solving problems the same way.

4
MOVING ABOUT
MOVEMENT AND MOTION

The movements of the human body and those of many other land animals rely on levers, pivoted by joints and moved by muscle power. This is a versatile system, but it places some severe limits on the speeds and distances that land animals can travel.

People have turned to other means of movement. Building boats enabled people to travel over the sea. It has, however, taken us thousands of years to develop mechanisms in our ships that can rival the sophisticated buoyancy control systems and water-tight compartments of ancient molluscs, whose construction is remarkably similar to that of the modern submarine.

Flight is a 20th-century human discovery, pioneered by insects, developed and discarded in some reptiles, which has reached the peak of perfection in birds. Almost all the principles of lift and control that are used in a modern airliner evolved in birds. Apart from wheeled landing gear and more power, we have added few refinements to their basic aerodynamic structure. Even jet propulsion has evolved on several independent occasions in the natural world.

The force that we can exert by moving our limbs is limited by the strength of our muscles, so humans have developed hydraulic power, a force already harnessed by the earthworm.

A bird's feather.

Trains and centipedes both have jointed sections, which allow them to travel round tight curves in tunnels.

PRINCIPLES OF HYDRAULICS

When force is applied to a liquid inside a rigid container, its volume does not get smaller. Instead, the force is transmitted (sent) through the liquid, so liquids inside pipes can be used to transmit forces over distances. A small volume of liquid, pumped through a narrow pipe, carries enough force to move a large object a short distance (as in the diagram below).

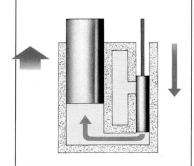

EARTHWORM TO LIFT

HYDRAULICS

Hydraulic forces are used in animals for two main purposes. Some invertebrates have a hydrostatic skeleton, where the fluid inside their body cavity controls their shape. Their body changes shape when muscles force fluid from one area to another. Hydraulic forces also move liquids around the body inside tubes. The heart pumps blood around our bodies.

LIFT

Hydraulic pressure is transmitted through small pipes to move heavy objects, such as lifts. Hydraulic fluid is pumped into the bottom of the cylinder to push the lift up. Fluid is then pumped out to move the lift down. Hydraulic forces are also used in machines such as hydraulic jacks, which allow cars and lorries to be lifted, so that wheels can be removed. Hydraulic crushers can transmit enough force to squeeze a scrap car into a solid block of metal.

▼ Starfish have rows of muscular, tubular feet spaced regularly along each arm. These are connected to a system of internal pipes that are filled with fluid. Hydraulic pressure forces fluid into the feet when muscles squeeze the pipes. A starfish creeps forward by extending, bending and retracting the feet in sequence, using waves of muscle-driven hydraulic power.

◄ Leaves are held in shape by turgor pressure, a hydraulic force that pushes against the wall of every cell. Leaves wilt when this force decreases and the cells collapse. (Right) The sensitive plant's leaflets fold up when they are touched because cells at their base lose water, so the pressure inside them falls and they collapse. The leaflets spread out again when these cells regain turgor pressure.

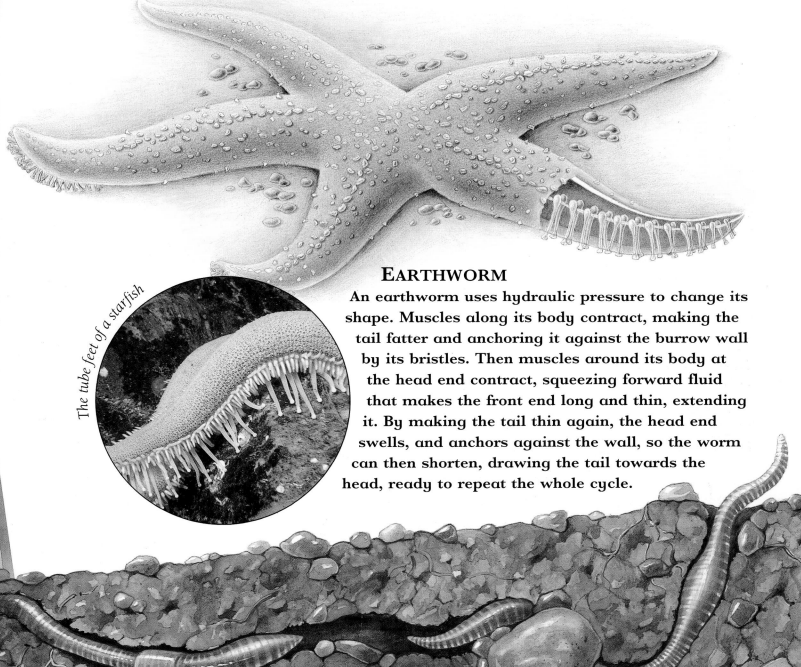

The tube feet of a starfish

EARTHWORM

An earthworm uses hydraulic pressure to change its shape. Muscles along its body contract, making the tail fatter and anchoring it against the burrow wall by its bristles. Then muscles around its body at the head end contract, squeezing forward fluid that makes the front end long and thin, extending it. By making the tail thin again, the head end swells, and anchors against the wall, so the worm can then shorten, drawing the tail towards the head, ready to repeat the whole cycle.

ALBATROSS TO GLIDER
GLIDING AND SAILING

Flight first evolved in insects, which use a system involving the rapid beating of wings by powerful muscles. Some midges have wings that beat up to 1,000 times per second. This system uses too much energy to lift large animals off the ground.

Aircraft exploit a less energetic principle, which evolved separately in birds and which depends on the aerodynamics of curved wing surfaces. Air flows faster over the longer, curved top of the wing, creating an area of low pressure. This causes the wing to move upward. This is the force we call lift.

ALBATROSS
Birds generate extra lift by flapping their wings and pushing down on the air. Broad wings are best for this. Gliding species, like the albatross, fly for long distances without flapping their wings. They have long and narrow wings.

Lift

Direction of air

▲ Birds' wings are curved above but flatter below. When air flows over this aerofoil shape it creates aerodynamic lift, because differences in air pressure are generated between the upper and lower surfaces. Higher pressure underneath the wing pushes it upwards.

◄ Velella velella, the By-the-Wind-Sailor, is a jellyfish that floats just below the ocean's surface. It is carried wherever the wind blows by its vertical sail, which is held above the water surface.

▼ Sails have an aerofoil shape and behave like vertical wings. When a boat is sailing into the wind, it is driven forward by differences in air pressure on opposite sides of the sail.

Direction of air

▼ *Wings on the earliest aeroplanes were made from a fabric skin stretched across a light framework, mimicking the construction of the wings of extinct pterodactyls.*

GLIDER

Gliders do not have engines. They can only fly if they are towed up into the air. The forward speed of a glider's wings generates lift, but glider pilots also search out columns of rising warm air, called thermals, to provide some of the lift that keeps their planes airborne. This technique is used by soaring eagles, which can reach high altitudes by riding on thermals.

PARACHUTING

Drag or air resistance slows falling objects, as well as slowing aircraft down as they move forwards. Plants have used parachutes that use this effect to spread their seeds for millions of years. The dandelion's plume of hairs slows its fall, so that the wind carries it further away from the parent plant. Rising currents of warm air even carry plumed seeds upwards, which explains the presence of dandelions growing on the parapets of high buildings. Human parachutists use the same principle as seeds, when air trapped under the parachute canopy creates drag and slows their fall. Modern parachutes can also be flown like a glider, and steered by spilling air from parts of the canopy.

◄ *Birds use their tails as rudders. Puffins, which have short tails, use their broad feet as well. Tails and feet can also act as air brakes, slowing the bird as it lands.*

▼ *Aircraft have movable surfaces on their wings and tail. These are used to change the direction of the flow of air so that the aircraft can turn or move up and down. The hinged surfaces are rigid and less manoeuvrable than the flexible tail of a bird.*

Movement of Rudder

Movement of Elevator

SQUID TO JET ENGINE
PROPULSION

Jet propulsion works by forcing gas or liquid under high pressure through a small nozzle so that the gas pushes against surrounding air or liquid, driving the container forward.

JET ENGINE

A jet engine sucks in air at one end and forces it out of the other at a much greater speed. Vertical take-off aircraft like the Harrier use jet engines with nozzles that direct the high-pressure exhaust from the engines down for take-off, but swivel to point backwards when the plane is airborne, so that it flies forwards.

▼ When a scallop is threatened by a starfish, the two halves of its shell snap shut, expelling a jet of water and propelling the animal forward.

SQUID

Squid use jet propulsion to drive themselves through the oceans. A squid's body contains a powerful elastic bag of contracting muscles that squeeze a jet of water out of a backward-pointing nozzle. The animal swims at up to **32** kilometres an hour when escaping from predators, sometimes even leaping out of the water and onto the decks of ships.

Jet propulsion is also used by people to propel objects out of containers. In jet-engined aircraft, the engines suck air in, forcing it into a chamber where fuel is burned. This chemical reaction produces hot expanding gases that shoot out and thrust the aircraft forward. Many fireworks, such as Roman candles, are also blasted into the air by a jet of hot gas. Explosives ignite in the tube and the glowing balls of burning chemicals are shot out of the tube, propelled by expanding hot gases. Different chemicals produce the colours.

▲ Puffball toadstools consist of a thin spherical skin packed with tiny dust-like spores that can grow into a new fungus. Raindrops falling on the skin force a jet of air out through a small hole in the top of the fungus. This jet of air carries with it a cloud of spores.

▼ The squirting cucumber grows along roadsides in southern Europe and disperses its seeds in a jet of liquid. Water pressure builds up in the balloon-shaped fruit, which separates suddenly from its stalk. Then the seeds are squirted out in a jet of sticky liquid.

Some animals that live in water use jet propulsion to move around, while some plants use the technique to disperse their seeds. People use jet propulsion mainly in aircraft. Power in jet engines is generated by using a fan to draw air in and force it into the chamber where the fuel is burned. The hot air is then forced out of a nozzle at very high speed.

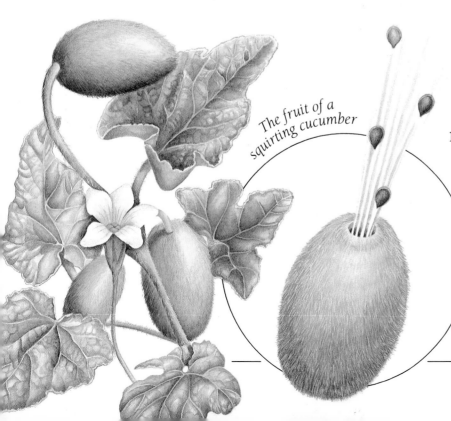

The fruit of a squirting cucumber

FISH SWIM BLADDER

Fish can control their density. By varying the amount of air in the swim bladders inside their bodies, they change their buoyancy so that it exactly balances their weight. Then they can float below the surface without rising or falling. Fish such as sharks, that do not have swim bladders, must swim constantly to prevent themselves from sinking.

Swim bladder

NAUTILUS TO SUBMARINE
BUOYANCY AND FLOATING

Objects only float if they are less dense than water. Then, the volume of water that they push aside weighs more than they do and pushes back with enough force to keep them afloat. Objects that are denser than water are heavier than the volume of water they displace (push aside), so they sink.

Dense, heavy objects can be made to float if bubbles of air are trapped inside them. Ships sink when water replaces the air inside their hulls.

NAUTILUS

The nautilus is a primitive marine mollusc that is related to squid and octopuses. Unlike these animals it has a shell, which is divided into a spiral series of buoyancy chambers. The animal lives in the outermost chamber. It fills the others with just enough gas to match its overall density with that of the surrounding sea water, so that it neither sinks nor floats upwards.

DIVING

Submarines float because the air in them makes them less dense than the water they displace. But they dive when water is pumped into tanks, increasing their density.

Tanks full

NAUTILUS CHAMBERS

A large nautilus shell contains about thirty chambers. Extra buoyancy chambers are added as the animal grows, to allow for its increased weight.

SUBMARINE

Submarines need to be able to float on the surface and dive beneath it. Compartments in a submarine's hull filled with air serve the same purpose as the nautilus's buoyancy chambers. The density of sea water increases in the deeper ocean, so a submarine's crew trims its buoyancy by pumping water in or out, to match the density of the sea water.

▶ The air trapped in coconuts makes them float. They are carried by ocean currents until the waves cast them up on tropical beaches, where they germinate. Their tough but light fibrous husk provides extra buoyancy and protects the seed from salt water.

▼ A lifebelt is a ring that can save the life of a non-swimmer who has fallen into the water. It is made of very low density material that has many air bubbles trapped inside it. It will remain afloat even when supporting the weight of a person dressed in water-logged boots and clothes.

◀ Vast numbers of tiny animals and plants live in the surface waters of the oceans. They are known as plankton, and all have developed methods of floating. The bubble raft snail floats just below the sea surface by creating a platform of bubbles to which it clings.

▶ Inflatable armbands provide just enough buoyancy to support a child learning to swim. Air can be let out of the armbands to decrease buoyancy as the child gains confidence, until he or she can swim unaided.

Wrenches, used by engineers to grip and tighten nuts and bolts, are mechanical versions of a crab's claw, an ancient natural tool. Strong muscles in the claw and rows of teeth on its jaws give it a firm grip, while the long arm acts as a lever.

5
HELPING 'HANDS'
USING TOOLS

Tools are devices that can be used to help in a particular task. Many animals have special parts of their bodies to help with tasks such as finding food. Some animals also use objects that they find as tools. In this way, they are like the early humans who caught animals and collected seeds and fruits. These early humans developed simple tools, like spears and axes, for hunting.

Later on people needed tools to sow, harvest and process crops. Farming provided reliable food supplies that supported larger populations in villages, towns and cities. Drills, saws, chisels, files and hammers were needed for building houses. In the 18th and 19th centuries new tools to cut,

shape and join iron and steel were developed, along with machine tools, which perform the same action over and over again, making large numbers of identically-shaped components. These led to the manufacture of the mass-produced objects, such as cars and household gadgets that we use today. Now we also use computer-controlled machines.

Claws of mantis shrimps are tools that stun and grip prey.

Throughout history, the basic tools we use have remained almost unchanged. Most have the sharp edges, fine points, grinding and rotating surfaces, meshes, nets, combs and hooks that have allowed animals or plants to perform similar tasks for millions of years.

Animals have evolved natural versions of all the tools that humans have combined into this penknife.

TOOTH TO CHISEL
SHAPING AND MANUFACTURING

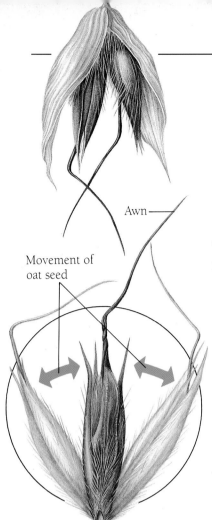

▲ *Oat seeds can plant themselves, thanks to a natural drilling mechanism. A long bristle-like structure called an awn is attached to each seed. Awns are made of a material that coils and uncoils as it dries out, slowly drilling the seed into the soil.*

Awn

Movement of oat seed

Animals solve the problem of cutting, shaping and drilling materials by using natural tools such as flat, sharp-edged teeth, rough tongues, and twisting and turning motions that push pointed objects through soft materials. Our chisels, files and drills provide very similar solutions to the same problems. Such simple tools have led to many of the most important advances in human civilization, from boat building to the construction of cities and machines.

BEAVER

The large incisor teeth of a beaver are the natural equivalent of the chisels used by carpenters to shape wood. Carpenters' chisels eventually wear away and need to be replaced, but the beaver's teeth are still in perfect condition after almost **20** years of constant chewing and tree-felling. Their teeth grow continuously from the base to make up for wear. They are also self-sharpening, thanks to differences in the hardness of the tooth layers, which always wear at different rates to leave a sharp edge.

The incisor teeth of a beaver.

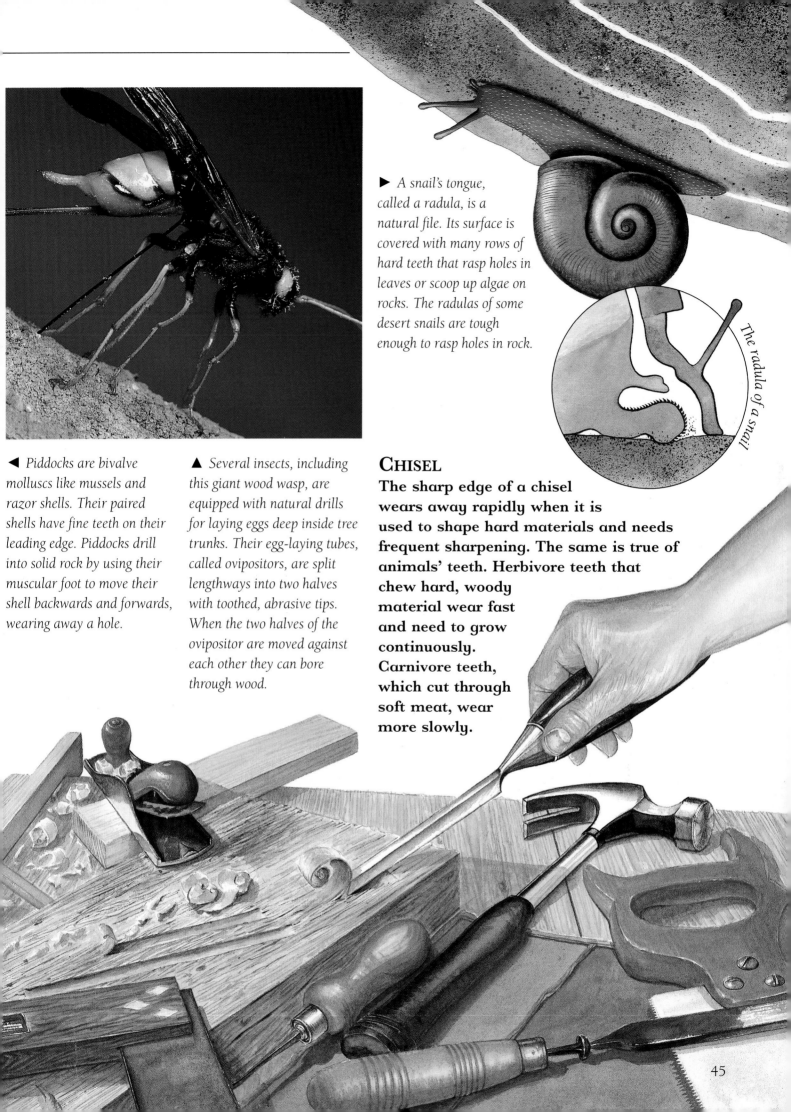

▶ A snail's tongue, called a radula, is a natural file. Its surface is covered with many rows of hard teeth that rasp holes in leaves or scoop up algae on rocks. The radulas of some desert snails are tough enough to rasp holes in rock.

The radula of a snail

◀ Piddocks are bivalve molluscs like mussels and razor shells. Their paired shells have fine teeth on their leading edge. Piddocks drill into solid rock by using their muscular foot to move their shell backwards and forwards, wearing away a hole.

▲ Several insects, including this giant wood wasp, are equipped with natural drills for laying eggs deep inside tree trunks. Their egg-laying tubes, called ovipositors, are split lengthways into two halves with toothed, abrasive tips. When the two halves of the ovipositor are moved against each other they can bore through wood.

CHISEL

The sharp edge of a chisel wears away rapidly when it is used to shape hard materials and needs frequent sharpening. The same is true of animals' teeth. Herbivore teeth that chew hard, woody material wear fast and need to grow continuously. Carnivore teeth, which cut through soft meat, wear more slowly.

CILIA

Mussels use a form of biological conveyor belt system for collecting food. The two halves of the mussel shell open when the tide comes in and the sea water covers the mussel. Tens of thousands of microscopic beating hairs, which are called cilia, create a current of water. The sea water contains minute food particles, which are trapped in sticky mucous that the mussel secretes over its cilia surface. The beating cilia then waft the food into the gut, for digestion.

CILIA TO CONVEYOR BELT
GATHERING AND COLLECTING

Sorting objects into different sizes is an important step in many processes. In mining, coal and mineral ores need to be broken up and graded into different sizes for specific uses. In the food industry, vegetables like mushrooms and potatoes are graded by size before they are sold. In most cases the easiest way to carry out the grading processes has been to copy nature, either by passing the objects through nets, grids and meshes of different sizes or by passing them through finer and finer combs.

The cilia of a mussel

▶ *Several species of caddis-fly larvae that live in slow-flowing streams, spin fine fishing nets that are attached to rocks. These behave like miniature trawl nets, filtering out fine food particles from the water.*

▼ *A trawl net acts like a giant sieve, filtering fish out of the ocean depths. The net's mesh size is adjusted to let small fish escape, so that they can continue to grow until they are large enough to be fished for economically.*

CONVEYOR BELT

Conveyor belts are important components of most factory production line systems. They are continuous belts, like giant rubber bands, that run around rollers and carry a steady stream of components to a point where they can be processed. Some airports have a similar systems called moving walkways for transporting people, where passengers stand on a conveyor belt that carries them to their flight departure point.

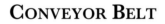

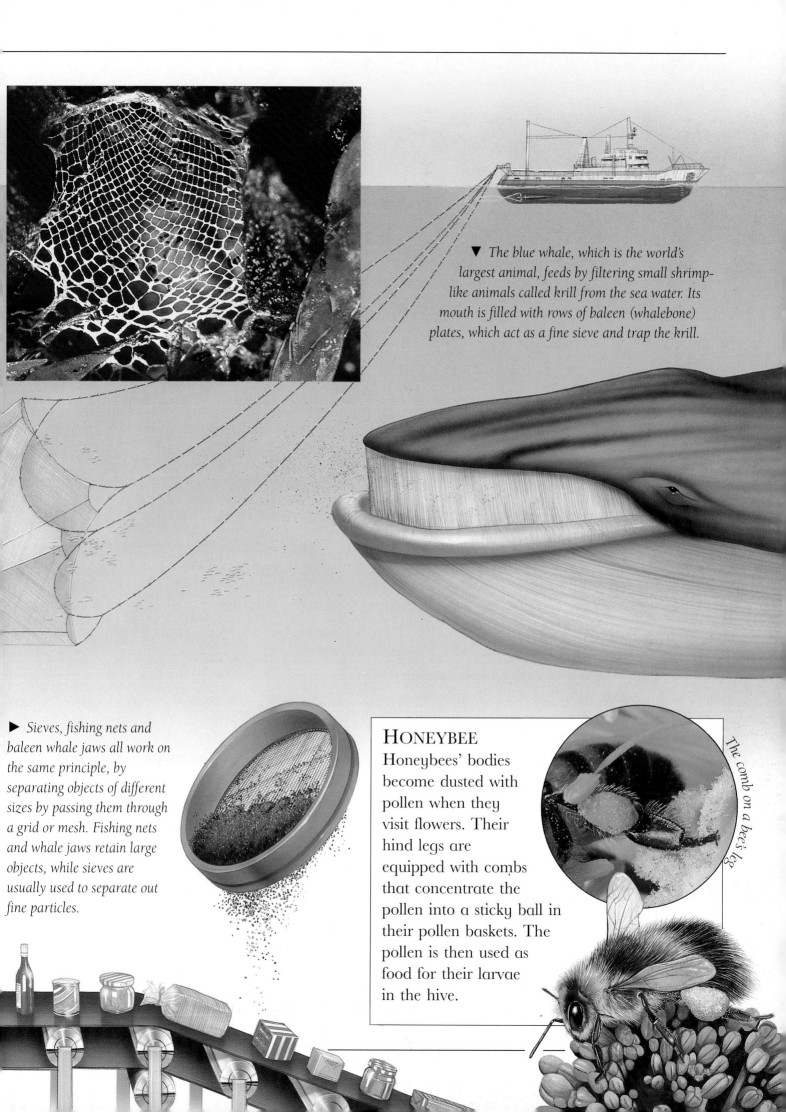

▼ The blue whale, which is the world's largest animal, feeds by filtering small shrimp-like animals called krill from the sea water. Its mouth is filled with rows of baleen (whalebone) plates, which act as a fine sieve and trap the krill.

▶ Sieves, fishing nets and baleen whale jaws all work on the same principle, by separating objects of different sizes by passing them through a grid or mesh. Fishing nets and whale jaws retain large objects, while sieves are usually used to separate out fine particles.

HONEYBEE
Honeybees' bodies become dusted with pollen when they visit flowers. Their hind legs are equipped with combs that concentrate the pollen into a sticky ball in their pollen baskets. The pollen is then used as food for their larvae in the hive.

The comb on a bee's leg

CROSSBILL TO SCISSORS
PINCERS AND TWEEZERS

Toothed jaws and birds' beaks may have provided inspiration for the invention of scissors, which are now used for everything from slicing through metal plate to fine micro-surgery in hospital operations. Objects cut into small pieces need to be picked up and human fingers are often not delicate enough for this task. Again, the natural tools used by animals have provided a solution. Fine tweezers and probes are little more than copies of the devices found on many small animals' legs.

CROSSBILL

The two halves of a crossbill's beak overlap at the tip, so that they act like a pair of scissors. The birds feed on pine seeds, and the shape of their powerful beaks is perfectly adapted to splitting the tough scales of a pine cone and then extracting the seeds that are hidden between them.

SCISSORS

Birds' beaks and the jaws of animals like fish and mammals open and close like a pair of scissors, pivoted on a hinge at one end. Powerful jaw muscles open and close the upper and lower halves, so that they cut or crush food. Scissors work in a similar way, except that they are pivoted on a screw and our fingers provide the force to close them. Our jaws work like giant scissors, armed with teeth.

PROBING BIRDS

Animals use their claws, jaws, and paws as natural tools to capture, cut up, and manipulate food. The Galapagos woodpecker finch behaves like a woodpecker, hacking holes in plants in its search for grubs. Unlike the true woodpeckers, this finch has never evolved a long tongue to probe for grubs. Instead it has learned to use a cactus spine to impale its prey.

▲ *The fine points of watchmakers' tweezers are designed to pick up and manipulate tiny screws and gear wheels. Even so, they are crude in comparison with the needle-sharp, pointed jaws of many insects.*

▲ *The jaws of a dragonfly nymph are attached to the end of a hinged structure that is normally folded beneath its head. The jaws extend with lightning speed when prey comes within reach, impaling its soft body between the needle-sharp points.*

▲ *The aye-aye is a primate that lives in Madagascar. Each hand has sharp, slender fingers, with an especially long middle finger which is used for grooming, scratching, and picking the teeth, as well as for probing for insects hidden in cavities in trees.*

▲ Human fingers are less specialized but more versatile than those of other animals. We must use small tools, like a dentist's probe, to adapt our fingers to special tasks. The probe is used to remove small particles of food and plaque that have stuck on the tooth's surface.

Plants cannot see but they can sense the direction that light comes from. Sunflowers detect the position of the Sun and their flowers turn to face it as it moves across the sky. The sunflower stem twists during the day and untwists at night.

6

GATHERING INFORMATION
SENSORS AND DETECTING

Our ability to explore our surroundings and to understand the other living organisms that we share them with has been assisted by the invention of instruments that extend the range of our senses.

Sound waves are vibrations that are reflected from the surface of objects but which can also enter them. This property has allowed scientists to develop machines that can locate small or distant objects from the echoes they reflect. In this way they can investigate structures that are normally hidden from view, such as oil deposits below the sea or an unborn baby in its

Solar furnaces generate high temperatures by focusing the Sun's energy into an oven that can reach 3,800°C.

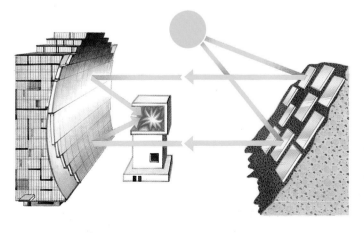

mother's womb. Many wild animals have senses that we do not possess. They can also detect wavelengths of light that are invisible to humans, but by developing special cameras and films we can extend our own vision. Perhaps it does not come as a surprise to discover that birds, which have migrated between continents in darkness and bad

Sunflowers focus the Sun's energy on their seeds.

weather for millions of years, can use built-in biological compasses to help them navigate. What is more surprising is that this system also seems to be present in primitive bacteria, but does not occur in humans. Even the simplest organisms seem to have senses that we lack. By understanding them, we may learn to develop new technologies.

DOLPHIN
A dolphin's head contains a fatty organ called a melon, which focuses sound waves into a sonar beam. Dolphins hunt shoals of fish by listening for echoes reflected from their prey. Dolphin sonar is sensitive enough to identify a single large fish within a shoal.

DOLPHIN TO SONAR
SOUND AND PRESSURE WAVES

Sound and pressure wave systems for detecting hidden underwater objects have developed rapidly in the 20th century. This is partly because of the threat of submarine warfare, but these technologies also have many peaceful uses. Sonar has allowed the mapping of our planet's sea floor. It can even be used to listen to the songs of whales.

WAVES
Vibrations travel in waves through air and water. This can be shown easily by touching the surface of water with a vibrating object such as a tuning fork. A pattern of waves instantly spreads out from the point. High-frequency waves, which produce high-pitched sounds, are closer and low-frequency waves are spaced out.

The melon in a dolphin's head

Melon

Brain

SONAR
Sonar stands for SOund Navigation And Ranging and uses sound waves to measure the position, speed and distance of underwater objects such as submarines. Active sonar involves generating a sound pulse and measuring the time taken for echoes from underwater objects to return. This allows their distance to be measured. If the sound pulse is sent out as a moving, narrow beam, then the direction and speed of the echo's source can be measured. Passive sonar does not send out sound waves, it listens to them. This system does not betray the presence of the listener.

ECHOES
Sound waves bounce off solid objects and send back echoes (sonar is also called echolocation). Sound travels at 1,500 metres per second in sea water, so if a sound pulse takes four seconds to bounce back to microphones in a submarine's hull, then the sea floor is 3,000 metres away.

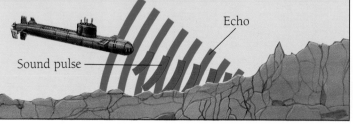

Echo

Sound pulse

▼ *Some bats emit high-pitched ultrasound, allowing them to hunt in total darkness. The ultrasound waves bounce back from any object that they hit and as the bat closes on its prey the returning sound waves increase in frequency. This allows bats to judge the distance of their prey as they close in for the kill, and to navigate safely in dark caves.*

▲ *Several moth species are able to detect the bat's ultrasonic squeaks and have evolved two methods for escaping from almost certain death. Some drop to the ground as soon as they pick up the first faint signals. Others confuse the bat's detection system by emitting high-pitched squeaks of their own. These interfere with the returning signal that guides the bat to its victim.*

▶ *Some fish have a very sensitive system for detecting underwater movements all around them. This consists of a lateral line canal along the sides of the fish. This tube or groove contains sensitive hairs and is open through pores to the outside water. Water movements caused by faint pressure changes and vibrations rock the hairs and generate nerve signals. In this way fish are aware of other animals nearby. We use mechanical vibration detectors, called seismographs, to detect earthquake tremors.*

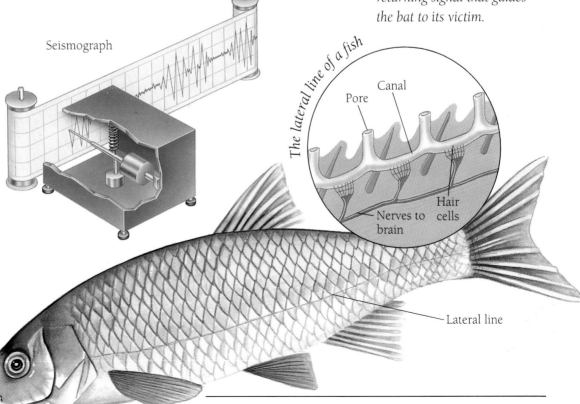

Seismograph

The lateral line of a fish

Pore

Canal

Nerves to brain

Hair cells

Lateral line

EYE TO CAMERA
LIGHT AND HEAT

Human eyes only detect radiation that lies within the light spectrum of a rainbow, which stretches from short-wavelength violet to long-wavelength red. We can use the longer wavelengths of infrared light by using infrared cameras. These form images in total darkness of warm objects that emit infrared. Many cameras that protect buildings against intruders at night work on this principle. We can also convert light into heat, by focusing its energy onto a very small surface.

◄ *Pit vipers are equipped with infrared sensors on either side of their jaws. These can form a thermal (heat) image of their prey in total darkness. Their victims are not aware that they are being hunted until it is too late to escape.*

► *Warm bodies emit infrared radiation which is invisible to the human eye. Infrared light can only be detected by special cameras and films, which give false colours to the different strengths of radiation that they record. As you can see, the centre of this camel is hotter than its outside.*

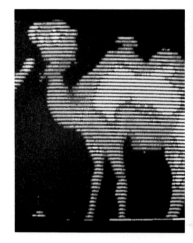

EYE

The eyes of vertebrate animals are almost spherical balls, which allow light to enter through a narrow hole in the front, called the pupil. A lens behind the pupil focuses light beams onto a light-sensitive layer of cells, called the retina, at the back of the eyeball. The retina cells are rods that are sensitive to dim light and cones that detect colour and bright light. Together they convert the image formed on them into electrical signals, which they send to the brain along the optic nerve. Eyes can adjust to changes in light intensity with an iris that surrounds the pupil. This uses muscles to open or close the pupil in dim or bright light. In the same way, a mechanical iris diaphragm is used to adjust the amount of light entering a camera.

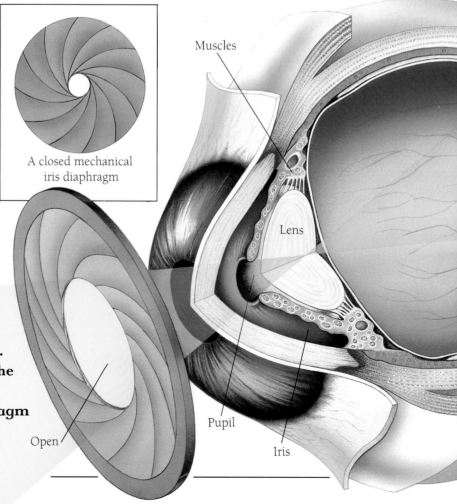

A closed mechanical iris diaphragm

Muscles

Lens

Pupil

Iris

Open

Bee's view

Flowers seen under
ultraviolet light

n's view

▲ The eyes of bees and some other insects can detect short-wave radiation in the ultra-violet part of the spectrum. This means that they see colours and patterns in flowers in a quite different way to humans, especially if the flowers reflect ultraviolet light strongly.

▶ Some flowers are sensitive to changes in light intensity, so that their petals close up at night and may even close when a dark cloud covers the Sun. This behaviour is thought to protect pollen from dew at night and from approaching rain during the day. (The daisy even gets its name from its opening and closing flowers – day's eye.) We use sensors that detect light intensity changes as automatic switches, to turn street lights on in evening twilight and to turn them off at dawn.

Optic nerve

Retina

CAMERA

Cameras are primitive, mechanical versions of vertebrate eyes. They are light-proof boxes, equipped with a lens to focus an image on film that is briefly exposed when a shutter is opened. In eyes the image is focused by changing the shape of the lens, but cameras are focused by changing the distance of the lens from the film. The film, coated with light-sensitive silver salts, corresponds to the retina. An iris diaphragm controls the amount of light entering the camera.

Film

Lenses

Light

Iris diaphragm

HOMING PIGEON

Scientists have found that homing pigeons get lost if magnets are attached to their heads. The pigeons navigate by orienting themselves to the Earth's magnetic field. They have a natural compass, a magnetic compound of iron oxide called magnetite, embedded in their neck.

HOMING PIGEON TO COMPASS
MAGNETISM AND GRAVITY

We use the Earth's magnetic field to navigate our way around the Earth's surface, to create accurate maps and to plot courses for travel between places. Exploring the Earth and space has depended on accurate instruments. Today we can travel thousands of miles by aeroplane and arrive at a precise destination with pinpoint accuracy.

COMPASS

The Earth has an iron core that behaves like a bar magnet which has its ends close to the North and South Poles. This core creates a magnetic field around the planet. A magnetized iron needle that is free to turn will always point north or south along the Earth's lines of magnetic force towards the North or South Pole. This is a simple compass.

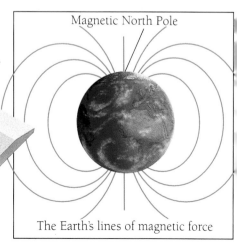

Magnetic North Pole

The Earth's lines of magnetic force

◀ The closely-spaced gills under a toadstool's cap are covered with spores, which drop down between the gills and are carried away in the wind. The toadstool's gills keep perfectly vertical by detecting gravity, so that their spores can fall freely between them. If the toadstool is tilted the gills quickly realign themselves Like living plumb lines, they are always perpendicular to the Earth's surface.

▼ Electrical fields can also be used to gather information. Metal detectors create electrical fields that penetrate the soil. Buried metal objects interact with the electrical field, and send a signal to the operator's earphones. Once an object is found it can be dug up and examined.

▶ A builder uses the effect of gravity on a plumb line (a weight on a fine cord) to help build vertical walls. Gravity pulls all objects directly towards the centre of the Earth, so the line is perpendicular to its surface.

◀ Magnetic compass termites of Australia build their nests almost on a North-South line, although they cannot detect magnetic fields. This makes best use of the Sun's heat. At dawn the flat east wall warms up quickly in the heat of the Sun. At noon, only the thin nest edge faces the Sun and at dusk the flat west face absorbs heat from the setting Sun.

▲ Sharks have special organs in their noses called ampullae of Lorenzini, which allow them to find prey that is completely hidden from view. These organs can detect the faint electrical signals produced by the twitching muscles of a fish that may be buried below sand. The shark then blows away the sand and grabs the hiding fish.

Several organisms, including this glow-worm, generate light energy in parts of their bodies by breaking down a chemical called luciferin. This light allows glow-worms to communicate at night, by flashing their lights on and off.

7
KEEPING THINGS GOING
ENERGY

Every action of animals and plants needs energy. Solar energy is captured by plant leaves and used by them to make sugars, proteins and fats. The plants are then eaten by herbivores and the herbivores, by carnivores, so the Sun's energy is passed along the food chain. We need energy to grow, to move and even to think.

Energy does not appear and disappear. It is passed around and converted from light to heat to electricity to sound and so on. Modern human societies are highly developed because we can store and transport energy. Like some other animals, we store seeds that contain energy captured from the Sun, for use when crops cannot be harvested.

But unlike animals and plants we use fossil fuels, such as coal, gas and oil, to produce heat, light and power. By burning the fuels we can release the energy that they contain. We often convert one form of energy into another form that is easier to use. For example, we make electricity which is easy to transport along power cables to the places where it is needed.

Some toadstools can produce light energy.

Humans now use so much energy that it is important to cut down wastage of energy, because it is expensive to produce and can often pollute the environment. The 'lost' energy has to go somewhere.

Humans can communicate at night by using illuminated signs.

SPRINGTAIL TO POLEVAULTER
RELEASING STORED ENERGY

Materials contain stored energy, which is called potential energy because it has the potential to be converted into other forms of energy, such as light and heat. We burn coal, oil and gas to convert their chemical energy into heat, and to generate electricity.

SPRINGTAIL

This tiny animal uses a lever, called a furcula, under its tail to polevault itself into the air. The springtail forces fluid into the furcula, which swells. When the furcula is released, it snaps straight, hurling the animal into the air.

POLEVAULTER

The energy of movement, called kinetic energy, generated during a polevaulter's sprint is converted to potential energy when the pole touches the ground. The pole bends, and when its natural elasticity begins to straighten it, it releases energy and hurls the vaulter over the bar.

The electric organ of an eel

▶ *Electric eels can carry a charge of up to 600 volts, which can stun a fish or even a person. Layers of muscle in its body act like the plates of a storage battery, accumulating an electric charge which the fish can release suddenly.*

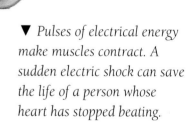

▼ *Pulses of electrical energy make muscles contract. A sudden electric shock can save the life of a person whose heart has stopped beating.*

The furcula of a springtail

Furcula

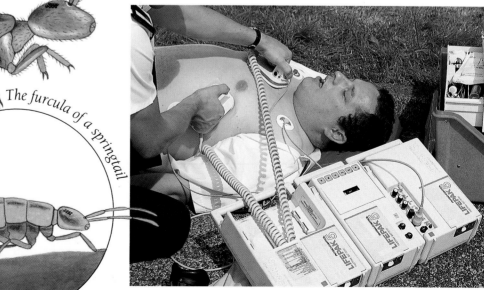

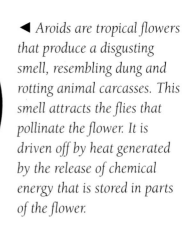

A thermograph of the aroid

◄ Aroids are tropical flowers that produce a disgusting smell, resembling dung and rotting animal carcasses. This smell attracts the flies that pollinate the flower. It is driven off by heat generated by the release of chemical energy that is stored in parts of the flower.

◄ Vegetable oil is a rich source of chemical energy that is often stored in seeds. About 70 percent of a Brazil nut is stored oil. This oil supplies the energy needed for growth when the nut germinates and produces a seedling.

▼ Oils contain chemical energy which is converted into heat and light energy when they are burned. Oil is easy to store and transport, which is why it is often used for heating and for generating power.

▼ Marathon runners pack their bodies with stored energy. They starve themselves for a few days before a race, then eat lots of starchy foods. This makes their muscles store extra glycogen, a carbohydrate that provides the chemical energy that powers their muscles.

SPIDER'S WEB

1. The sticky spiral thread of a spider's web is covered with a liquid secreted by the spider. The force of surface tension draws this liquid into round droplets pulling in a coil of silk thread at the same time.

The silk threads of a spider's web

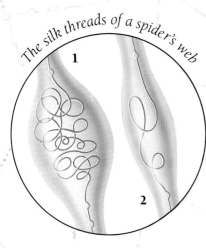

2. When a fly collides with the web, the initial impact is absorbed by the silk in the droplets. The silk is reeled out so that the thread gets longer without breaking. Once the fly has been killed, surface tension pulls the droplets and the web back into shape.

SPIDER'S WEB TO AIRCRAFT CARRIER
ABSORBING ENERGY

Fast movements are often essential for survival in the natural world. Catching prey can depend on a quick lunge and a short, violent struggle. Escape from enemies requires instant acceleration. But the shock of such sudden movements can damage delicate tissues unless the energy of movement – called kinetic energy – is absorbed when the animal stops suddenly. Natural systems have evolved to absorb kinetic energy, protecting delicate organs and tissues with springs, elastic structures and energy-absorbing materials. People who travel quickly, by bicycle, car or plane, depend on similar solutions to protect them from collisions and sudden speed changes.

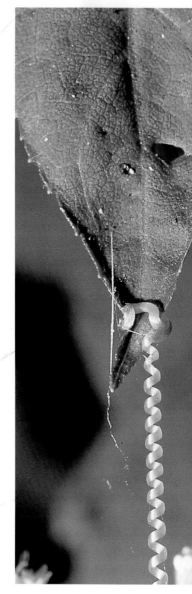

▲ *As soon as tendrils of climbing plants like vines and cucumbers touch an object, they begin to coil around it. Once attached, the tendril then coils into a spring, which acts as a natural shock absorber when the plant is buffeted by the wind.*

◀ *Male big-horn sheep settle disputes over mates and territory with head-to-head encounters. The rams head-butt each other with great violence, until one challenger is subdued.*

▼ *Nowadays, most cyclists wear safety helmets, which will protect their heads if they fall off their bicycles. The helmet absorbs the shock when the cyclist's head hits a hard object.*

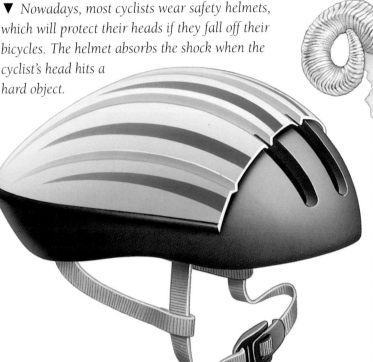

AIRCRAFT CARRIER

Arrestor wires are stretched between two reels across an aircraft carrier deck. An aeroplane, landing at 240 kilometres an hour and weighing 10 tonnes, is brought to a safe halt because the extending wire absorbs its kinetic energy, just as the thread of a spider's web cushions the impact of a colliding fly.

SOFTENING THE BLOW

Many animals need to protect their brains from damage during their normal life. The brain of a big-horn sheep (see above) is protected by a bony shield, called an ossicone, which absorbs the energy from blows. A cyclist's safety helmet uses a similar system of energy absorption, preventing skull fractures and brain damage in a collision.

Woodpeckers bore holes in wood to find food and build nests. The bill hits the wood at about 20 kilometres an hour. The force that the skull experiences is 250 times that which an astronaut feels on lift-off. An ordinary brain would quickly be reduced to pulp by this pounding, but the woodpecker's brain is protected by very dense bone that acts as a shock absorber.

EIDER DUCK

Birds' feathers keep them warm as well as enabling them to fly. Eider ducks have soft, downy chest feathers, which they use in their nests to prevent the eggs and young from becoming chilled. Eider down is one of the best natural insulators, trapping layers of warm air.

EIDER DUCK TO DUVET
KEEPING WARM

Our bodies generate heat energy when we digest food, and one of the best ways to keep warm is to stop that heat from escaping too quickly. We can do this by wearing extra layers of clothes, so that each successive layer traps another layer of warm air. This way of preventing energy loss is called insulation.

DUVET

A duvet keeps you warm while you are asleep because it is filled with insulating materials that trap layers of warm air. This insulation slows down the loss of heat from the body. The same principle is used in the production of outdoor clothing that is designed to protect mountaineers and polar explorers from freezing.

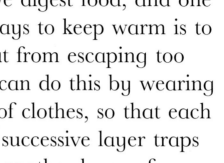

◀ *Animal fur usually consists of hairs of several different lengths. These trap layers of warm air just above the skin, reducing heat loss. Some animals have thick, insulating coats that enable them to survive in harsh alpine and polar habitats.*

SYNTHETIC FIBRES

Large amounts of eider down were once collected for making bed quilts, and animal furs were used for clothing, but today synthetic materials are usually used instead. These are made from crude oil and can be spun, woven and moulded into a wide variety of products. Synthetic fibres are often stronger than natural ones and are not damaged by fungi or insects.

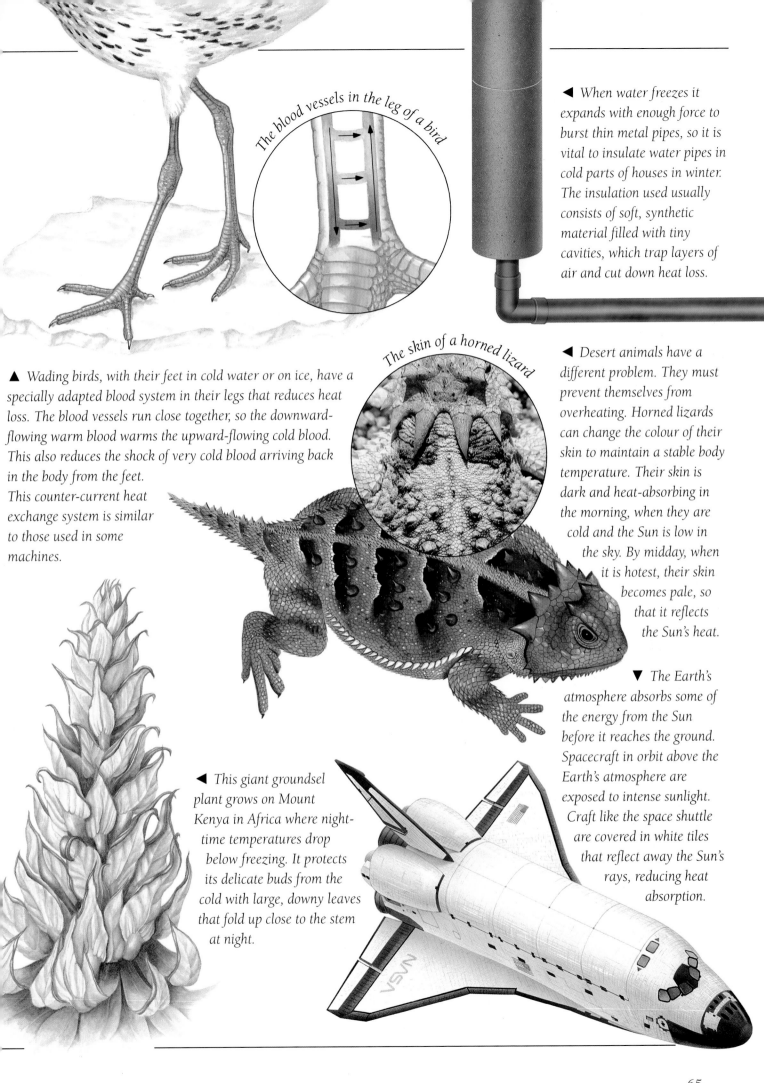

The blood vessels in the leg of a bird

◄ When water freezes it expands with enough force to burst thin metal pipes, so it is vital to insulate water pipes in cold parts of houses in winter. The insulation used usually consists of soft, synthetic material filled with tiny cavities, which trap layers of air and cut down heat loss.

▲ Wading birds, with their feet in cold water or on ice, have a specially adapted blood system in their legs that reduces heat loss. The blood vessels run close together, so the downward-flowing warm blood warms the upward-flowing cold blood. This also reduces the shock of very cold blood arriving back in the body from the feet. This counter-current heat exchange system is similar to those used in some machines.

The skin of a horned lizard

◄ Desert animals have a different problem. They must prevent themselves from overheating. Horned lizards can change the colour of their skin to maintain a stable body temperature. Their skin is dark and heat-absorbing in the morning, when they are cold and the Sun is low in the sky. By midday, when it is hottest, their skin becomes pale, so that it reflects the Sun's heat.

▼ The Earth's atmosphere absorbs some of the energy from the Sun before it reaches the ground. Spacecraft in orbit above the Earth's atmosphere are exposed to intense sunlight. Craft like the space shuttle are covered in white tiles that reflect away the Sun's rays, reducing heat absorption.

◄ This giant groundsel plant grows on Mount Kenya in Africa where night-time temperatures drop below freezing. It protects its delicate buds from the cold with large, downy leaves that fold up close to the stem at night.

Sunlight

CHLOROPLAST TO SOLAR CELL
LIGHT AND ELECTRICITY

Light is a clean, free form of energy. Plants use energy from sunlight by capturing it with natural solar cells called chloroplasts. We store solar energy captured by solar cells as electricity in batteries.

Chloroplasts in leaf cells

Sunlight

SOLAR CELL

A solar cell converts light into electrical energy. The cell's low power output means that it must be used in large numbers. But, unlike stored energy sources such as oil, gas or batteries which eventually run out, solar cells provide power output indefinitely, for as long as the Sun shines on their surface. This makes them the ideal power source for instruments on spacecraft, because the solar cells can provide power during flights that may last for many years. Batteries would be far too heavy and would not last long enough to perform this task.

CHLOROPLAST

The cells of leaves are packed with lots of chloroplasts, which contain chlorophyll. This allows light energy to break down water molecules, converting the energy into chemical energy in a process called photosynthesis.

Solar cells

An insect in a Venus fly trap

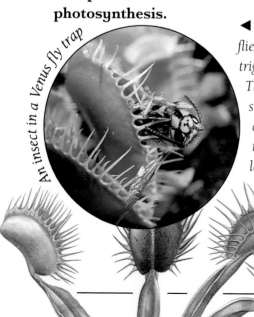

◀ *Venus fly trap leaves catch flies when the insects touch trigger hairs on their surface. These act like electrical switches, triggering the flow of water out of cells along the leaf midrib, so that the leaf snaps shut.*

▶ *Electrical switches operate by breaking a circuit and stopping the flow of an electric current through a wire. When the switch is turned on, the circuit is completed and electric current begins to flow through the wire again. Animals and plants also use 'switches' to start or shut off the flow of an electrical current carrying a signal to another part of the organism.*

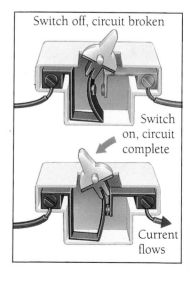

Switch off, circuit broken

Switch on, circuit complete

Current flows

► Nerve fibres carry messages from the brain to muscles and other organs, and bring messages from the body back to the brain. The outside of the nerve fibre is covered with a fatty material called myelin, which stops the electrical signal leaking away into the surrounding tissues. Myelin acts in exactly the same way as the plastic insulation surrounding an electric cable.

▼ Wires need to be insulated, to make them safe to touch and to prevent the electricity flowing away. Plastics are good insulators, because they are tough and durable, and do not allow electric current to flow through them. So most electrical wires have a thick, flexible plastic coating.

Myelin

▼ People have developed optical fibres of transparent glass which are covered with a material that acts as a mirror. Light beams are reflected down through the optical fibres' core. The fibres can be bent easily, so light can be shone around corners into awkward places. Fibre optics are used to carry coded messages, in the form of pulses of light.

► The fur of a polar bear behaves like a natural optical fibre, conducting light energy down to its dark coloured skin. Here the light is converted to heat and absorbed, so keeping the bear warm in the cold Arctic climate.

Light beams

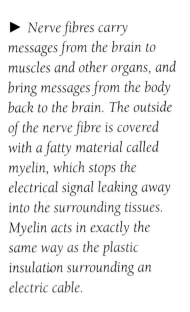

▼ Plants also make use of optical fibres. Fenestraria lives in the South African desert with its leaves almost completely buried below the sand. This protects them from water loss and from grazing animals. Each leaf tip is transparent, allowing light to enter and travel down the leaf, so photosynthesis can take place.

Both light and electrical energy can be converted into other forms, such as the chemical energy produced in photosynthesis. Light and electricity can also travel along wires or tubes carrying their energy with them. For example, nerve fibres, are like living wires that conduct electrical signals.

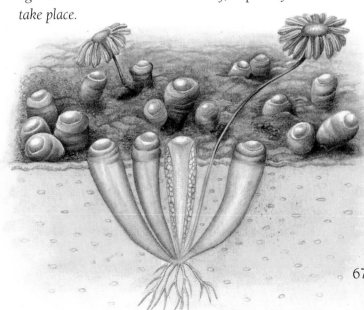

Farmers use chemicals to kill weeds that would compete with their crops for water and minerals. These desert shrubs prevent competition for water by producing natural chemicals that prevent seeds germinating too close to them.

8
MARVELLOUS MIXTURES
LIVING CHEMISTRY

Plants and animals are living factories that can turn simple chemicals into more complex molecules. The most important of these are called proteins. Some proteins are used directly to make parts of the plant or animal cells. Others, called enzymes, are used as chemical tool kits, to break down and rebuild molecules into new types that are used for special purposes. Some animal enzymes break down food and convert it into other chemicals that are used during growth. In plants some enzymes join carbon dioxide and water to make molecules called carbohydrates that are used for making cell walls.

Modern science uses many molecules from organisms. Often they can be extracted from the plant or animal that makes them, but in many cases scientists have learned how the molecules are constructed and can make them in a laboratory. The drug aspirin, which is used to cure headaches, was first discovered in willow twigs, but now is made artificially.

The types of protein that an animal or plant produces are controlled by chemical codes, called genes, inside cells. Each gene makes a different kind of protein. The latest scientific advances allow researchers to switch genes on or off inside cells, or even to cut genes out of one organism and put them into another. This process will allow us to develop completely new ways of using the chemicals that living organisms produce.

Pyrethrum plants have natural insecticides in their cells.

Artificial chemicals protect our crops from harmful pests.

LEAF

A leaf is coated with a thin, waxy cuticle that makes it waterproof. This is essential because carbon dioxide for photosynthesis is absorbed from the air spaces between the leaf cells. If these fill with water, photosynthesis would slow down. In hot, dry climates the cuticle also prevents water loss from the leaf, and the plant.

LEAF TO SHOE
PROTECTING SURFACES

Surfaces need to be protected from water, grit and even bright light. Polishing cars and furniture, oiling cricket bats and wearing ultraviolet-absorbing sunscreen lotions are all ways of protecting surfaces from wear and tear. Animals and plants produce chemicals in their cells (secretions) which they use to protect their surfaces.

Purple Alpine leaves

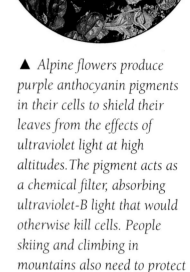

▲ *Alpine flowers produce purple anthocyanin pigments in their cells to shield their leaves from the effects of ultraviolet light at high altitudes. The pigment acts as a chemical filter, absorbing ultraviolet-B light that would otherwise kill cells. People skiing and climbing in mountains also need to protect their skin from the UV light.*

◄ *Ducks' feathers are coated with an oily secretion that prevents them from becoming waterlogged when the duck dives under the surface for food. The water droplets roll off the duck's back when it surfaces, keeping the feathers dry and the bird warm.*

▼ *The shiny wing cases of beetles have a hard outer coating, or cuticle, which is waterproof and protects them from damage. The insect cuticle is reinforced with a protein called sclerotin, which makes it one of the toughest materials made by animals.*

SHOE

Shoe leather is made from the hides of cattle. Natural oils are produced in the living animal's skin, keeping it supple and waterproof. Once the hide is made into a shoe it dries, hardens and loses its water-proofing. Grease is rubbed into leather to keep it soft and waterproof.

◄ *Varnishing wooden surfaces protects them from dirt and scratches and water seeping into the soft wood. Early varnishes were made from natural oils and secretions from insects that used the same substances themselves.*

SUNDEW

The sundew is an insectivorous plant whose leaves are covered with stalked glands tipped with droplets of adhesive. The droplets look like nectar and attract insects, which become stuck as they touch them. Then the leaf secretes enzymes that dissolve the insect, and the plant absorbs its nutrients.

SUNDEW TO STICKY TRAP
ADHESIVES

Adhesives, ranging from the starchy plant extracts that we lick on the back of a postage stamp, to the powerful synthetic glues that are used to stick windscreens onto motor car bodies, are an essential part of modern life. Without adhesives, much of our world would quite literally fall apart.

A leaf stalk falls from a twig

a sundew leaf

STICKY TRAP

Sticky sundew leaves provide the inspiration for a safe and easy way to destroy pests that infest crops. The sticky trap is made from a strip of yellow plastic that is coated with a layer of glue. Many insect pests are strongly attracted to the colour yellow and land on the trap, where they become stuck to its surface and die. This is a method of pest control that does not use toxic chemicals, unlike insecticide sprays, which sometimes kill harmless insects.

▲ *Cells in plants are glued together with a natural adhesive called pectin. When leaves begin to fall from the trees in autumn an enzyme called pectinase is produced where the leaf stalk joins the twig. This dissolves the pectin glue away, until eventually the leaf falls from the tree, leaving a scar that is protected by the remains of the pectin glue.*

▼ *Holes in punctured tyres can be temporarily sealed by covering them with liquid rubber, which dries to a hard skin when it makes contact with air. This allows the tyre to be partly inflated again, so the motorist can drive to a garage.*

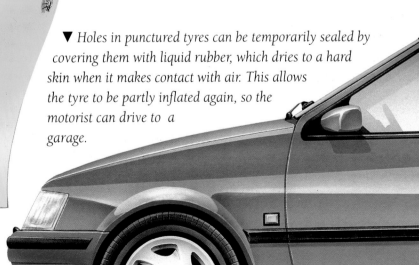

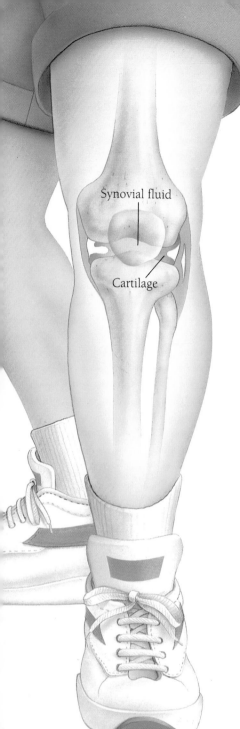

Synovial fluid

Cartilage

KNEE TO ENGINE
LUBRICANTS

When people rub their hands together on a chilly winter's morning, they are using friction to generate heat. Friction between surfaces produces energy. When you rub your hands the force of the friction produces heat energy, but the force of friction also makes surfaces wear away. Pencils leave a mark on paper because of friction.

Friction is a constant problem for animals, because it wears out their moving parts and because energy is needed to overcome friction between moving surfaces. Animals rely on lubricants to reduce wear and to cut down the energy needed for movement. We use lubricants on moving parts in machines for exactly the same reasons.

ENGINE
We reduce friction in machines by using oil or grease to lubricate their moving surfaces. If the oil level in an engine and gearbox is allowed to drop too far, friction between rapidly moving parts will cause wear and overheating. Wheel bearings must also be greased, to reduce friction and allow free movement.

KNEE
Joints between bones would soon wear out unless they were lubricated. Friction in joints like the human knee is reduced by a covering of smooth cartilage on their surfaces, which are enclosed in a cavity filled with lubricating synovial fluid.

◄ Snails move on a large, muscular foot that is propelled by waves of muscle contraction. They can glide easily over rough surfaces like stone and concrete because their foot secretes mucus as a lubricant that reduces friction and prevents the foot's soft surface from wearing away. The mucus dries as silvery trails, which show where snails have passed in the night.

BROKEN CELLS TO BROKEN PIPES
ANTIFREEZE

Pure water freezes at 0°C but its freezing point is lowered if other substances are dissolved in it. Sea water freezes at a lower temperature than fresh water because dissolved salt lowers its freezing point. Ice formation is a constant hazard for organisms in cold climates, because ice crystals expand as they form, destroying cells. Animals overcome the problem by accumulating antifreeze chemicals in their tissues, lowering their freezing point. We use the same principle to prevent freezing of machine cooling systems in cold climates.

BROKEN PIPES
Antifreezes are added to car engines in winter to prevent water freezing in the cooling system. The expanding ice can split pipes, burst radiators and damage engines. More antifreeze must be added in colder climates, to lower the freezing point of the water even more.

BROKEN CELLS
1. When large ice crystals grow in cells they kill them by bursting through the delicate cell membranes. Antifreezes can prevent ice formation, but other protective measures have also evolved.
2. Some beetles can tolerate freezing because their blood contains special chemicals that encourage the formation of minute ice crystals that are too small to damage their cells.

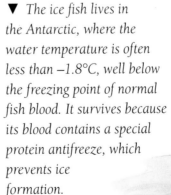

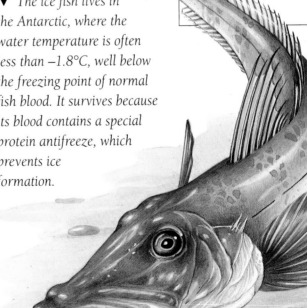

▼ *The ice fish lives in the Antarctic, where the water temperature is often less than −1.8°C, well below the freezing point of normal fish blood. It survives because its blood contains a special protein antifreeze, which prevents ice formation.*

▲ *The American tree frog (Hyla versicolor) hibernates in the leaf litter on forest floors, unlike most frogs which overwinter in ponds. It can survive freezing of up to 65% of its body water because it accumulates an antifreeze called glycerol in its blood, and this protects delicate organs from ice crystal formation.*

▲ *Today we use chemicals to kill insect pests that attack crops. Genetic engineers hope to provide crops with a powerful self-defence system against their pests.*

NEW IDEAS FROM OLD
GENETIC ENGINEERING

Genes are made of a molecule called DNA (deoxyribonucleic acid). DNA is a chemical code that controls the type of proteins made in cells, and so the characteristics of all living things. Genetic engineers have learned to understand this chemical code and can cut and rejoin pieces of DNA, so that they can exchange genes between bacteria, animals and

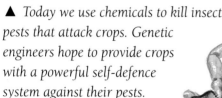

Scorpion cell

1. An organism is found whose cells carry a gene that produces a toxic protein which can kill insect pests. This might be another plant or an animal, such as a scorpion.

2

2. The toxin gene is found on a long DNA molecule, in the cell nucleus. The DNA is extracted.

Toxin gene

3

3. Special enzymes that cut DNA are used as chemical scissors, to snip out the piece of DNA that contains the toxin gene.

4. This small piece of DNA is then transferred into a bacterium that joins it to its own DNA molecules.

Bacterium

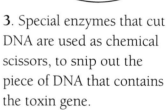

Long DNA molecule

4

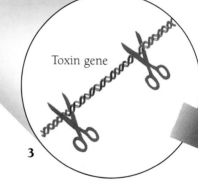

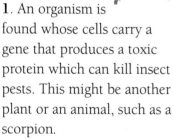

▲ *Many crop plants can be damaged by frost when ice crystals form inside their cells (see page 73). One way to protect the crops is to provide them with antifreeze genes from fish that swim in ice-cold Antarctic seas. These genes make proteins that stop ice crystals forming in the fishes' blood. The proteins also stop ice forming in the plant cells.*

▶ *Leeches make a protein called hirudin, which prevents blood from clotting so that they can drink blood from their victims. Hirudin is useful in medicine because it stops dangerous blood clots forming after patients have had operations. Genetic engineers hope to make hirudin cheaply in plants by transferring leech genes into them.*

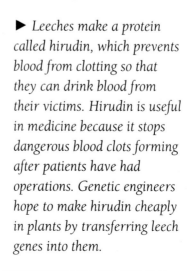

plants. This knowledge allows them to create organisms with useful new characteristics.

Scientists have created a new biotechnology industry by learning how living organisms work and by inventing methods for changing them. We all hope that genetic engineering will help us to grow more food, and provide new and more effective cures for diseases.

▲ *Plastic litter does not decay, so it can pollute the environment for centuries. Some bacteria make molecules that can be used to manufacture biodegradable plastics that slowly break down into water and carbon dioxide. Now genetic engineers have moved the bacterial plastic genes into plants, which can make plastic molecules in large quantities.*

BIOHAZARD

Scientists are now providing plants and animals with genes that allow them to make new chemical products. We must be careful that engineered genes do not spread into wild bacteria, plants and animals, which may damage the environment or create new pests and diseases.

Biohazard symbol

◄ *Poisonous chemicals have to be disposed of carefully. Scientists hope to add into plants the human genes that capture and destroy poisons that enter our bodies. These plants can then be grown on poisoned land and destroyed, along with the chemicals they have trapped.*

6

5

5. The bacterium infects a plant and transfers its DNA into the plant cells that have been grown in a laboratory. These cells are grown on a chemical that only lets cells with toxin genes develop into new plants.

6. The new plants are now protected by the toxin in their leaves, which kills caterpillars that begin to eat. The crop is safe for people to eat because we destroy the toxin when we digest our food.

GLOSSARY

Adaptation a part of a living organism that makes it better suited to its environment. For example, wings are an adaptation in birds and insects which enables them to fly.

Aerodynamic anything related to the flow of air over surfaces.

Aerofoil wings have curved surfaces above and below. This shape is called an aerofoil and generates lift when air flows over it.

Atom the smallest part of a chemical element that can exist on its own.

Axis an imaginary line through an object, that divides it into two halves.

Bacteria tiny, single-celled organisms. Some bacteria cause disease, but many are useful because they break down and recycle dead organisms.

Biodegradable something that can be broken down by bacteria and other living organisms.

Buoyancy the ability of an object to float.

Camouflage colours, patterns or shapes that make objects and living things difficult to see against their surroundings.

Carbohydrate a chemical compound of the elements carbon, hydrogen and oxygen. Carbohydrates include sugars and starch. They are made by plants during photosynthesis and are used to make plant cells. They are also used by plants and animals to store energy.

Carnivore an organism that eats animals.

Characteristic the appearance or function of a thing that enables it to be distinguished from other things.

Chemical bond the bond that holds atoms together in a chemical compound. Energy is released when chemical bonds are broken.

Chemical element a substance that cannot be broken down into simpler substances. Elements combine to form compounds. There are over a hundred different elements.

Chemical energy the energy that is released when chemical bonds are broken. This often happens when substances are burned or broken down by enzymes.

Chlorophyll the green compound in plant leaves, which they use to capture energy from sunlight.

Chloroplast a tiny structure in a leaf cell that contains chlorophyll.

Civilization the way in which people live together in organized communities.

Clotting the way in which blood dries on the surface of a wound, preventing further bleeding.

Conduction the transfer of energy through substances. Heat energy is transferred by conduction from hot parts of a substance to cold parts. Electrical energy (a current) is transferred through materials that conduct electricity.

Convergent evolution when two organisms independently evolve the same adaptations in response to the same needs. Butterflies and birds have both evolved wings for flying, but this is convergent evolution because birds have not evolved from butterflies. They have separately arrived at the same solution to the same problem.

Density the weight of a specific volume of a substance. A bag of coal is heavier than the same sized bag of feathers, because coal is denser than feathers.

Elastic able to bend or stretch when a force is applied. An elastic material returns to its original shape once the force is removed.

Electron a particle that orbits around the centre of an atom. Electrons carry an electrical charge. When electrons flow through a wire, they produce an electric current.

Embryo a very early stage in the development of a plant or animal.

Environment the surroundings of an organism.

Enzyme a protein that splits other molecules into smaller, simpler parts.

Evolution the way in which all forms of life change as time passes. The individuals of a species are all different. The ones with the most useful features survive best and have most young. These young resemble their parents and so carry the same useful features, which they pass on to their young and so on. In this way the features of a species will change over time. It has evolved.

Foliage the leaves that cover a plant.

Food chain a sequence of organisms, where each one is eaten by another. Plants are at one end of food chains and are eaten by herbivores. Carnivores are at the other end of food chains, because they eat herbivores.

Force something that pushes or pulls an object in a particular direction.

Frequency the number of occasions that something happens in a period of time. Sound travels as waves of energy. In high frequency sound lots of waves are produced in a very short time.

Gene a particle inside a cell that controls the characteristics of living organisms. For example, the colours of eyes and hair are controlled by genes. Each gene controls the production of a particular protein.

Genetic engineering the process of artificially moving genes between organisms that are distantly related, in a way that would be impossible in nature. For example, human genes can be put into plant cells by this technique.

Germination the beginning of growth in a spore or an embryo inside a seed.

Gravity the force that pulls objects together. The most obvious effect of gravity is to pull objects towards the centre of Earth.

Grazer an organism that eats pieces of growing plants.

Herbivore an organism that eats plants.

Hydrostatic skeleton the fluid that fills the hollow body cavity of animals such as worms, and controls their shape.

Incubation eggs will not hatch unless they are kept warm. Most birds incubate their eggs by sitting on them.

Insectivore an organism that eats insects.

Insulation a material that does not conduct heat, electricity or sound.

Invertebrate an animal that does not have a backbone or internal skeleton. Some invertebrates have a hard outer covering, called an exoskeleton, instead.

Larva the young stage of an animal that is different to the adult stage. For example, a caterpillar is the larva of a butterfly.

Molecule a group of atoms of an element or compound that exist on their own.

Mollusc one of the main groups of animals. Snails, slugs, oysters, octopus, cuttlefish and squid are all molluscs.

Nutrient any one of a number of substances that are essential for the growth and survival of organisms.

Nymph an early stage in the development of some insects, such as dragonflies. Nymphs shed their skins several times before becoming adult insects.

Organism all living things are organisms – plants, animals and fungi.

Photosynthesis the process by which plants use the energy from sunlight to break down water molecules into hydrogen and oxygen. The chemical energy produced in this reaction is used to make sugars from carbon dioxide in the air and water taken up through the roots of the plant.

Pollen the male cells of flowers, which must join with female egg cells before seeds can be formed.

Pollination the transfer of pollen from a flower to the female parts of another flower, where it joins with an egg cell to form a seed that then germinates.

Pollution the waste products which we produce that damage the environment and organisms living in it.

Predator an animal that hunts other animals (the prey) for food.

Pressure the force pushing against the surface of an object.

Protein a chemical compound found in meat and seeds. Our bodies use protein that we eat for growth and repair.

Skeleton the framework of a body which provides support and protection. Some animals have external skeletons, such as shells, and others, like us, have internal skeletons of bone.

Species a particular kind of organism.

Spectrum the visible colours of light that we can see. It consists of the colours of the rainbow – violet, indigo, blue, green, yellow, orange and red.

Spore one of the tiny cells that are released from fungi, which will germinate and grow into a new fungus.

Starch a carbohydrate which is often used to store energy in living organisms.

Surface tension the force that keeps drops of liquid such as water together. The tension gives the effect of an elastic skin on the liquid.

Synthetic anything that is made by people from simple raw materials, which are used to make complicated molecules.

Technology the practical use of science to provide materials and objects for use in industry and daily life.

Toxin a substance that kills living things.

Ultrasound very high frequency sound.

UV-B light high energy ultraviolet light that comes from the Sun and can damage living cells. We are usually protected from UV-B by the ozone layer in the upper atmosphere, but more UV-B now reaches Earth's surface because the ozone layer is damaged.

Vegetable oil oil that is produced in plants. Vegetable oils are an energy source in seeds and are extracted and used by humans in cooking.

Vertebrate an animal that has a backbone and an internal skeleton.

Wavelength some types of energy, such as sound and light, travel as invisible waves through the air. The waves have peaks and troughs, like the waves in the sea. The distance between the peak of one wave and the peak of the next is the wavelength. Different types of sound and light energy have different wavelengths. Red light, for example, has a longer wavelength than blue light.

INDEX

ACKNOWLEDGEMENTS

The publisher would like to thank the following for kindly supplying photographs for this book:

Endpapers *l*Oxford Scientific Films (O.S.F.)/Deni Bown, *r*Mary Evans Picture Library; page 4–5 Planet Earth Pictures; 6 O.S.F./Deni Brown; 7 *r*Harry Smith Collection, *b*Mary Evans Picture Library; 8 Bruce Coleman/Dr Eckart Pott; 9 *t*Phil Gates, *c*O.S.F./R.L. Manuel; 10 N.H.P.A./Jim Bain; 11 Biofotos/Heather Angel; 12 O.S.F./Alastair MacEwan; 13 *cr*S.P.L. *b*Bruce Coleman/N. Schwirtz; 14 Bruce Coleman/Dr Eckart Pott; 15 *b*Robert Harding/ Walter Rawlings, *r*O.S.F./Howard Hall; 16 *t*Bruce Coleman/J. & D. Bartlett, *b*N.H.P.A./N.A. Callow, *bl*Life Science Images/Ron Boardman; 17 Bruce Coleman/Jan Taylor; 19 *t*N.H.P.A./A.N.T. *b*O.S.F./Derek Branhall; 20 *l*N.H.P.A./A.N.T. *t*N.H.P.A./Stephen Dalton; 21 Planet Earth Pictures/Richard Coomber; 22 O.S.F./Kjell Sandved; 24 O.S.F./Daniel J. Cox; 25 *l*Bruce Coleman/Jane Burton, *r*O.S.F./Herbert Schwind; 26 *l*Bruce Coleman/Hans Reinhard, *r*Bruce Coleman/Kim Taylor, *b*Life Science Images/Ron Boardman; 27 N.H.P.A./Anthony Bannister; 29 *t*N.H.P.A./Anthony Bannister, *b*N.H.P.A./Norbert Wu; 31 *t*O.S.F./Zigheszczynski, *c*Bruce Coleman/J. & D. Bartlett, *b*O.S.F./Mantis Wildlife; 32 Bruce Coleman/Kim Taylor; 35 *t*Bruce Coleman/Adrian Davies, *b*N.H.P.A./Trevor McDonald; 36 O.S.F./Kathie Atkinson; 37 O.S.F./Kenneth Day; 38 O.S.F./G.I. Bernard; 39 N.H.P.A./ Stephen Dalton; 41 *t*O.S.F./Tom Ulrich, *b*O.S.F./Kathie Atkinson; 42 O.S.F./Kathie Atkinson; 45 N.H.P.A./Stephen Dalton; 46 Bruce Coleman/Andrew Purcell; 47 *t*Bruce Coleman/ Dr Frieder Sauer, *b*N.H.P.A./Anthony Bannister; 49 O.S.F./Konrad Wolhe; 50 Bruce Coleman/Atlantide; 51 Bruce Coleman/Hans Reinhard; 53 O.S.F./Stephen Dalton; 54 S.P.L.; 55 Bruce Coleman/Jane Burton; 56–57 Frank Lane/Tony Wharton; 57 Robert Harding/ Dr D. R. Harris; 58 Bruce Coleman/Peter Hinchcliffe; 59 *r*Bruce Coleman/Michael Price, *b*Robert Harding/G. R. Richardson; 60 S.P.L.; 61 *t*Biofotos/Paul Simon, *b*Allsport/Gray Mortimore; 62 O.S.F./Kjell Sandved; 63 O.S.F./Ray Richardson; 64 N.H.P.A./Dr Eckart Pott; 65 Bruce Coleman/G. Ziesler; 66 *c*S.P.L. *b*O.S.F./Kathie Atkinson; 68 O.S.F./Waina Cheng; 69 Bruce Coleman/J. Fennell; 70 *t*Harry Smith Collection, *l*Bruce Coleman/Kim Taylor; 71 Bruce Coleman/Jane Burton; 72 N.H.P.A./Stephen Dalton; 74 *t*N.H.P.A./Brian Hawkes, *b*O.S.F./Kathie Atkinson; 75 *t*Bruce Coleman/Stephen Bond, *c*N.H.P.A./John Shaw.

The publisher would like to thank the following artists for their contribution to this book:

Louise Boulton 35*c*, 40*b*; Robin Carter (Wildlife Art Agency) 29*rc*, 70*bl*; Richard Draper 26–27*t*/*bc*, 28*tl*/*b*, 29*tc*/*br*, 34*c*, 48*b*, 49*tr*, 51*b*, 54–55*b*, 55*tr*, 71*cl*; Angelika Elsebach 12*t*/*r*, 13*lc*/*br*, 27*br*, 34–35*b*, 62*bl*, 63*tc*, 73*bl*/*br*; Wayne Ford (Wildlife Art Agency) 28*tr*; Chris Forsey 66*tl*, 67*tr*/*cl*, 74–75; Mark Franklin chapter symbols 9*c*, 13*tc*, 17*c*, 19*c*, 27*c*, 30*tr*/*cl*, 39*tr*, 41*c*, 53*c*/*cr*, 60*c*, 61*tc*, 62*cl*, 65*tr*, 66*br*, 73*tr*, 75*tr*; Sally Gooden (Wildlife Art Agency) 8*l*, 39*bl*, 44*tl*, 61*c*, 65*bl*, 66*bl*, 67*br*; Ray Grinaway 10*tl*, 11*cr*, 44*bl*, 47*br*, 53*b*, 57*br*; Tim Hayward (Bernard Thornton Artists) 25*tc*/*c*; Adam Hook (Linden Artists) 16–17*b*, 41*br*; Ian Jackson 33*cr*; Roger Kent 69*b*; Paula Knock 64*bl*, 67*c*; Adrian Lascom (Garden Studio) 38*c*; Alan Male (Linden Artists) 30*tl*, 30–31*b*, 43*cr*, 45*tr*, 60*bl*, 65*c*; Maltings Partnership 56*bl*; Shane Marsh (Linden Artists) 44–45*b*, 49*b*, 70*br*; Josephine Martin (Garden Studio) 44*tr*, 49*cr*, 60*cr*, 65*tl*; Alex Pang 10–11*b*, 33*b*, 40*tr*, 40–41*c*, 46–47*b*, 47*t*/*c*, 52, 57*tr*/*tc*; Bernard Robinson 20*b*; David Russell chapter symbols 63*cl*; Guy Smith (Mainline Design) 8*c*, 8–9*t*, 9*r*, 11*tl*/*tc*, 31*tr*, 71*br*, 72–73*t*; Simon Tegg 36*br*, 37*cr*, 38*tl*; Ian Thompson 24–25, 25*bl*; Richard Ward 11*tl*/*b*, 12*bl*, 13*c*, 62–63*b*, 65*br*, 66*c*, 72*tl*; Alan Weston (Kathy Jakeman Illustration) 36–37, 37*br*; Joanna Williams (B L Kearley) 60*t*, 64*cr*; Ann Winterbotham 18*bl*, 19*br*, 23*br*, 26*tl*/*tr*, 27*cl*, 53*tr*, 54*t*, 55*tl*, 71*tr*; David Wright (Kathy Jakeman Illustration) 16*tl*, 17*br*, 18–19*t*/*b*, 25*br*, 48*t*, 70*c*.